A THOUSAND
MOUNTAINS
A MILLION HILLS

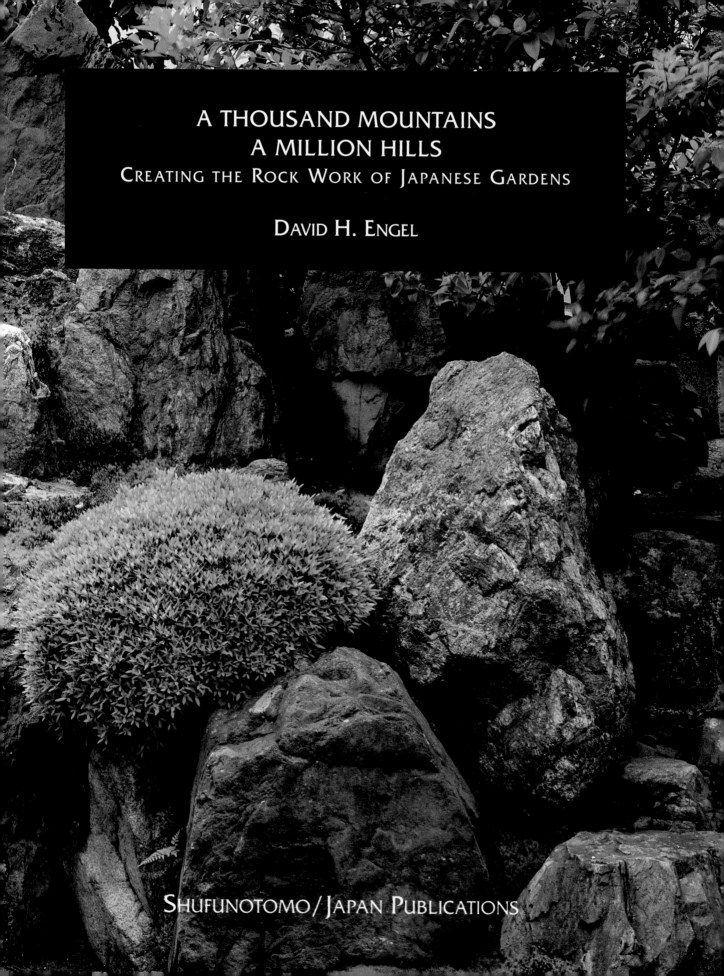

A THOUSAND MOUNTAINS
A MILLION HILLS
CREATING THE ROCK WORK OF JAPANESE GARDENS

DAVID H. ENGEL

SHUFUNOTOMO/JAPAN PUBLICATIONS

For Sano-sensei,
who taught me to see

Grasses and trees
look different
and the auspices look good.
Puffs of cloud
delight in trailing
around the peak.
A thousand mountains
a million hills
look up to
its virtue.
Is there anyone
who has never been blessed
with its shelter?

—*Musō Soseki*

ACKNOWLEDGMENTS

I acknowledge with gratitude the editorial criticism
of Dennis H. Piermont of LANDGARDEN;
the leads to Japanese and Chinese poetry and prose
provided by scholars Burton Watson and Hiroaki Sato;
the guidance through the gardens of Kōko-en at Himeji Castle
by its designer, landscape architect Makoto Nakamura;
and the line drawings by Anne Wilfer.
I thank also Allan Stoops of Ōtsu, who showed me
gardens of exemplary rock and stone work.

Jacket and Book Design by Jean Mahoney

First printing, 1995

Published by Shufunotomo Co., Ltd.
2-9, Kanda Surugadai, Chiyoda-ku, Tokyo, 101 Japan

DISTRIBUTORS
United States: Kodansha America, Inc., through Farrar, Straus & Giroux, 19 Union Square West, New York, NY 10003.
Canada: Fitzhenry & Whiteside Ltd., 195 Allstate Parkway, Markham, Ontario L3R 4T8.
United Kingdom and European Continents: Premier Book Marketing Ltd.,1 Gower Street, London WC1E 6HA.
Australia and New Zealand: Bookwise International, 54 Crittenden Road, Findon, South Australia 5023.
The Far East and Japan: Japan Publications Trading Co., Ltd., 1-2-1 Sarugaku-cho, Chiyoda-ku, Tokyo 101.

Printed and bound in Japan   ISBN 0-87040-969-7

NOTES 1. The garden of Kōko-en at Himeji Castle was designed by Prof. Makoto Nakamura, head of the
Department of Landscape Architecture at Kyoto University.

2. The author designed and supervised construction of the following gardens featured in this book: Nikko
Hotel, Chicago; Gulf States Paper Corporation, Tuscaloosa, Alabama; Fountainhead Corporate Park,
Tempe, Arizona; and the private gardens in Ridgefield and Greenwich, Connecticut; North Castle,
Ellicottville, Westchester and Putnam Counties, New York; and Moosehead Lake, Maine.

3. Photographs on the front and back covers and pages 2–3 are courtesy of Katsuhiko Mizuno; page 21 is
courtesy of Sekai Bunka Photo. All other photographs were taken by the author.

4. Chinese words are rendered according to the pinyin system.

5. Names of Japanese historical figures are written family name first. Names of persons from 1868
onwards are written Western order. Hyphens have been added to some names for ease of pronunciation.

CONTENTS

CHAPTER ONE

WHY ROCKS IN A GARDEN?

Our earth, wrapped in its thin skin of air, soil, water and plants, is essentially a ball of rock whirling through space. But, despite its apparent hardness, this mass of rock is paradoxically our nurturing mother—*yin* in Asian cosmology, the soft, receptive, female half of creation. Everything we see, all that exists, has its origins in the rock, our terrestrial home.

No wonder, then, that man has always derived comfort from being in contact with the earth's bare bones. We feel awe at the grandeur of views of the Grand Canyon, or Mount Everest, alpine peaks, the Rocky Mountains, and all the imposing heights and deep valleys of the world. Yet we also feel kinship and a degree of understanding toward those solid, exposed parts of our mother earth, compared to the enigma, the mystery, we sense on turning our eyes upward for a look at the heavens. After all, compared with the solidity of earth, infinite space is still far beyond our grasp. This, despite trips to the moon and unmanned space probes exploring our solar system. It is on earth where we feel permanence, protection and stability, and this is provided by the earth's chief ingredient: rock and stone.

We know that even the soils which sustain life-giving plants are merely rock pulverized and decomposed by the forces of wind, water, ice, chemistry and bacteria. With evidence of these processes before our eyes, we sense a bond of familiarity, on both conscious and unconscious levels, whenever we touch bedrock. We are fascinated to observe an excavation for construction of deep cellars and basements; crowds often gather around such work. In New York City, for instance, there is always a group of lingering passersby who cannot resist peeking through openings in construction fences to watch blasting operations and excavations into the bedrock of Manhattan schist.

This is more than just idle curiosity. Rather, we are drawn to the wonder of watching the peeling back of the thin patina of soil and man-made cover to reveal the underlying rock. Equally riveting is the bare rock face of a declivity cut into the side of a hill to make way for a road. There, revealed for the first time, is layer upon layer of bedrock, often metamorphosed, be it ancient basalt or sedimentary. It is akin to being allowed to descend into the depths of the earth, traveling back through eons of time. It is like watching a curtain being lifted to reveal a process that

Grand Canyon, Arizona

took place millions of years ago.

We respond to the stimuli of rock not only through our eyes, but also tangibly, feeling with our hands, and through our feet when we walk over it. Or, we may respond with our whole body, lying down on a rock surface or leaning against a vertical rock face. Perception of rock may come, too, from its smell, particularly when wet.

There is also an intellectual dimension to rocks. They are reminders, telltale signs of the forces of nature—wind, water, ice, sun—offering indisputable evidence of the passage of time. And it is time over the long haul: years, centuries, epochs, eons. Every age is there, exposed for all who have eyes to see. Rocks are a storybook, a historical record waiting to be read—and appreciated. How can one not feel awe on coming into contact with such venerable, solid structures from the past?

The same feelings of awe and appreciation are derived also from contact with those parts of rock that have become separated from their bedrock home, either by the forces of nature or by man. These rocks or boulders can symbolize the whole substratum, a solid connection to the spectacular mountain landscapes of the earth, whose farthest corners nowadays are visited and explored. Later we return home with memories, evoked perhaps by photographs, which we feel compelled to view again from time to time.

But there exist more solid, though modest, reminders—often unexpectedly encountered. I recall that moment when walking through a pasture on my farm I spied ahead a wide area of exposed bedrock, partly covered with lichens and

Deep ravines and swirling torrents.
Taroko Gorge, Taiwan

tatters of moss. But also there, plainly and deeply scratched in the hard granite surface, was a series of parallel lines running in a north-south direction. What had dug those furrows into the rock? I wondered. Obviously, they were not man-made. It had to be something heavy that had pressed down as it slowly moved along.

Then it came to me. This had been an area heavily glaciated; mile-thick sheets of ice had passed over the land thousands of years earlier. I reasoned that there had been rocks embedded in the ice, rocks harder than my exposed outcropping. And, like a diamond stylus, they had cut into the bedrock as they moved at a glacial pace. I was thrilled to encounter on my land this sign, this greeting from long ago. How wonderful it would be, I thought, if this bit of outcropping could be just detached from the earth and installed in a garden. I would then be able to see it and appreciate its message every day. It would be a link with the past, a daily reminder of the passage of time, of which I am increasingly aware as I grow older. What I felt that day, the longing to place that rock in some intimate corner of my life where daily I could view it, was essentially the same motivation that over the centuries, I believe, led garden builders in China and Japan to make rocks play such a necessary role in their gardens.

This attraction to stone and rock is sweetly and fancifully expressed in the following lines by the modern *haiku* poet Hōsai Ozaki in his book *Right under the Big Sky, I Don't Wear a Hat.*

Near the beach about two and a half miles away to the west of the town of Tonoshō, there is a village whose name is written "Sengen." But the island

Ancient metamorphosed lava flows between sedimentary layers exposed in a massive rock cut along a highway. *Highway 684, Westchester County, New York*

Limestone rocks as found in nature before removal for placement in a garden. *Kerrville, Texas*

In this *tsubo-niwa,* the very simplicity and sparseness of elements suggests the stringency of Zen. The standing rock, with its small, low, base rock in front and slightly off to the side, becomes an abstract mantra for a meditator. The camellia tree in the foreground brings the right occult balance to the scene. *Daisen-in, Daitokuji, Kyoto*

people call it "Senge." It is the source of extremely good stones, and those wonderfully big stones that make up the walls of Osaka Castle, which astonish everyone, are said to have been all carried from this island, through the sea of Senge. Even now, if you look at picture postcards, you see a great many large stones lying about, row upon row, just as they were thrown out on the coast, rather than taken away. That this island is made mostly with stones, that it is rich with stones of very good pedigrees, is oddly pleasing to me.

Ordinarily I root for small, insignificant pebbles lying about on the road. A pebble that happens to get kicked away by the front tip of your wooden clog and has gone out of sight someplace, or a pebble you kicked at and missed and that lies there silently as if it just popped out—they are so touching. Why do I feel a deep affection for such insignificant pebbles? The reason may lie somewhere in the fact that, kicked, trampled upon, or whatever is done to them, they remain wordless, silent. Because stones can't talk, they have no choice but to remain silent, yes. But, are stones that can't talk dead? I don't think so somehow. On the contrary, I think all stones are alive. Stones are alive. No matter how small the pebbles, they are alive, positively pulsating. Being alive, their silence increases its significance. People often speak of the quietness of silent grasses and trees, but I cannot agree with them. Grasses and trees do talk. When the wind begins to blow, when the rain begins to fall, they at once turn into extreme chatterers, don't they? But how about stones? Let the rain fall or the wind blow, they simply keep silent. Yet they are alive.

In a tougher vein, reflecting on the peculiar solace offered by a contemplation of stone, the American Scott Russell Sanders wrote:

There is nothing like geology to take the urgency out of the morning's news. If we could watch events from the rock's point of view, all of human history, *from the stalking of woolly mammoths to the launching of space shuttles, would appear like a blinding flash. Our longest running shows, such as Egypt or China, would be mere buzzings in the ears of stones.... Rocks won't keep much record of our brief transit. For all our drilling and blasting, we have barely scratched this stony planet.*

Oriental garden rock work, though, may seem an esoteric subject. Indeed, I am often asked how I, an American landscape architect, became so deeply immersed in the garden art of Asia—particularly of Japan. The answer begins in childhood in my family's gardens where, like a sponge, I eagerly soaked up every bit of lore I could learn about plants. I was always experimenting, moving garden features around, trying to create effects with trees and shrubs alone. But even then I can recall feeling that there was something missing, some solid, enduring element, though I was not sure what. I realized, at least, that evergreen trees and shrubs alone could not fill the void. At that point in my life, though, gardening was only a hobby.

Then came 1950, the Korean War, a turning point. Working for the military in Korea and Japan, I had the chance to encounter for the first time the powerful rock work in Japanese gardens. Their evocative arrangements revealed to me possibilities I had never before dreamed of. I sensed that, perhaps, I had at last found the missing element. I decided then and there to try to learn more about Japanese gardens, particularly the rock work. This inspiration, with all its ramifications, influences to this day my approach to landscape design, even projects that are simply contemporary gardens.

Several years later the opportunity

came. I was awarded a grant from the Japanese Ministry of Education to study landscape design at a Japanese university. With that backing, I was registered at Tokyo University of Fine Arts in a program which included the noted architect Junzō Yoshimura as one of its supervisors. Sometime later, Professor Yoshimura recommended that, as the most important part of my training, I enter an apprenticeship with a master landscape architect in Kyoto, the ancient capital and center of garden arts.

And so, with happy expectations I headed south, and began with Tansai Sano, my *sensei* (teacher), two years of learning. I was led by *sensei* along a path to garden construction in which nature, the prime inspiration, was coupled with my own creative instincts. And beyond gardens, Mr. Sano, the scion of many generations of garden artists and a truly universal man, introduced me to the other Japanese arts of painting, calligraphy, poetry, music, architecture, to folk customs, food, and also to Shinto and Zen Buddhism. Eventually, though all too soon, I returned to America, feeling bolstered and enriched with insights that from then on would affect both work and daily life. What stands out so powerfully in my memory is Sano-sensei's frequent insistence that I feel free when designing gardens. "Don't be held down by tired, outworn ideas and

I cannot help thinking that these hoary rocks are really a group of novices clustered around a venerable monk (the tallest of the rocks) raptly listening to his teachings. Within the gentle precincts of a Zen temple they are sheltered by a crape myrtle tree in flower and a Japanese maple. *Daitokuji, Kyoto*

practices," he would say.

For me, brought up within a culture essentially derived from European traditions and untouched by Asian metaphysics, my fascination with stone and rock really stemmed only from a simple love of nature. Imagine, then, what a jolt I felt on meeting the cultures of China and Japan, where people feel such close kinship with nature. This is colored by the influence of Buddhism, as well as by the even more ancient cults of Taoism and Shinto, whose precepts are suffused with an animism and mysticism born in the haze that obscures the dawn of civilization.

That kinship with nature, woven into the fabric of the lives of Asian peoples, shows up powerfully in all components of their cultures, particularly in their feelings when viewing natural landscapes. The Chinese painter and critic Zong Bing (375-443) loved rocky landscapes. They "have a material existence and yet reach into a spiritual domain," he wrote. Their "peaks and precipices rising sheer and high, the cloudy forest lying dense and vast…[have brought a] joy which is of the soul."

The Chinese poet Bai Juyi [Po Chü-i] (772-864) also wrote of the spiritually uplifting power of nature when describing his mountain retreat:

The poet has come to set these things first of all: to lift up his eyes and see the mountains; to lower them and listen to the stream; to look about him at

The seven rocks in this *karesansui* garden symbolize mythic elements in the Buddhist cosmogony: the standing rock in the far corner represents Horaisan, a mountain paradise supposedly located off the coast of China. The two rocks to the right and rear symbolize the crane island, *tsurushima,* and the two rocks in the center oval of moss (shown under snow) represent the tortoise island, *kameshima,* carrying the world. Folklore aside, the disposition of the rocks is purely an abstract design, balanced in the ground plane and creating new spatial volumes. The composition of these rocks on the gravel-covered plain immediately produces a sense of greater space, further enhanced by the raked furrows. *Ryōgintei, Daitokuji, Kyoto*

bamboos, willows, clouds and rocks, from morn till nightfall. One night's lodging brings rest to the body; two nights give peace to the heart; after three nights the drooping and depressed no longer knew either trouble. If one asked the reason, the answer is simply—the place.

The Song painter Guo Xi (1020-1090) focused more on the active interpretation that mountain landscapes demand:

Wonderfully lofty are these heavenly mountains, inexhaustible is their mystery. In order to grasp their creations, one must love them utterly, study their essential spirit diligently and never cease contemplating them, and wandering among them, storing impressions one by one in the heart.

It was this sense of nature as a free spirit that drew the Japanese, too, to wild and rocky mountain landscapes. Their native Shinto animism found in the Taoist exaltation of nature a confirmation, or at least a reflection, of their own regard for mountains, rivers, trees and rocks, believed to be the abodes of puissant *kami* (spirits or gods).

Musō Soseki, Zen priest, poet, garden-maker and mountain-wanderer of thirteenth-century Japan, described the free spirit called forth by the mountains in his poem "Lover of Mountains":

Your compassionate mind
soars like a summit.
There is your true effortless nature.
Some places smooth and gentle,
some places rugged and unapproachable.
The mountain has no wish to be
looked up to.
It is only people
who look up
in wonder.

For Buddhists, rocks symbolize Shumisen, a legendary holy mountain lying at the center of the world. This captivation with mountains and rocks remains today, despite being domesticated in Japanese gardens.

An awareness of this Asian fascination with nature, particularly mountains and rocks, and an understanding of the historical, religious and folkloric underpinnings of Asian gardens will aid the Western garden builder in his own work with rocks.

The object of this book, though, is to show rock work that stirs the feelings and evokes the wide world of nature, rather than to advocate making Japanese gardens. We can learn from Japanese principles of rock placement without deep attachment to Oriental traditions and legends. Indeed, some principles expressed in Oriental gardens are applicable anywhere. And, strange as it may seem, some of the recondite and arcane links to religion and philosophy may also be grounded in principles of optics and the psychology of visual perception.

This book deals with the employment of rocks in man-made landscape settings, using Japanese (and sometimes Chinese) ideas which can be applied in the West. It is about creating within a limited area scenes with the feeling of far-off mountains, waterways and distant hills.

Yet the question arises: Why put rocks in a garden? Aside from any purely physical or functional purpose, is there an unspoken need to be reminded of mountains? What about the people of the plains who have never seen mountains or rock exposed to view—the bare bones of the earth? It is not too far-fetched to believe that mountains, or their suggested representation in the form of rocks in a man-

The rocks, symbolizing islands emerging from a stormy sea, lead the eye to a soaring peak in front of the clipped hedge. The natural forms are manipulated into repeating and varying patterns of horizontals, verticals and diagonals, establishing an abstract composition. The sheared, mounded form of the tree suggests hills farther away. The low, moss-covered, attenuated mounds suggest even more distant archipelagoes. Because of their low-lying position, seeming much farther away than the rocks, they create a tension between the two opposing perspectives within this temple garden. *Zuihō-in, Daitokuji, Kyoto*

made landscape, can represent for them the world, its very beginnings, its origins, its seat of the gods. And therefore the desire emerges to be close to that divine element, that numinous entity.

Or following a line of thought that is less involved with divine origin, rocks and mountains represent solidity; they are the unchanging element of the environment when every living thing shows obvious and radical change—plants, animals, ourselves. Rocks may even be seen to symbolize some benign guardianship.

In material terms, of course, rocks predate the formation of soil, and therefore become a solid structural element in a garden. They barely change during our lifetime, while we may even appreciate those subtle accretions of time which are evident: lichens, moss, darkening of surfaces, patinas. Witness, for example, the Japanese love of *sabi* and *wabi*.

Rocks are found in such a variety of shapes, forms, textures and colors that they are capable of suggesting any number of landscape forms. It is as if Nature and the garden builder are given the opportunity to become partners in a process (or is it a game?), an intellectual enterprise to create a work of art in a garden which is not only aesthetically pleasing, but also embodies a spiritual content. It is a private conversation between the garden builder and his God or muse. And if there can be a benign spirit within a rock, welcoming into a garden brings its auspiciousness into the owner's life and home.

Having once felt the spiritual content of natural rock, one cannot help but reject the artificial. There is a difference in effect between a natural rock and a man-made one. The concrete, fiberglass, or plastic impinges upon the unconscious as well as the conscious mind of the viewer. It is the difference between what is genuine, honest and sincere and what is false, showy or tricky; between the fruits of steady, hard toil and those of fast gain by dishonest manipulation. Aging does not occur on fiberglass, and lichens do not grow there. It is the difference between walking on artificial green-colored turf and on a grass lawn. An artificial rock simply has not gone through the eons of existence (experience?) of a granite boulder. It shows no weathering and conveys no sense of age or the passing of time. No matter how realistically contrived, it is hard to imagine a spirit finding a home in a concrete or fiberglass boulder.

In the end, it is what the viewer perceives or feels as he observes the rocks, not how they look, or how cleverly they are composed. Does he feel deceived, cheated or dissatisfied by artificial rock? Does he sense its superficiality and its newness?

Natural rocks and stone bring strength, timelessness and a sense of the world's natural landscapes into a garden. They act, too, as links between the house, garden and the site itself. Rocks are honest, straightforward and natural, without affectation or pretense. When you look at rocks, you know that what you see on the surface runs through to the very heart of the material. This, in itself, is reassuring.

Rocks, forming cheek walls along garden steps, overlap each
other to make ins and outs, as well as pockets for plantings of
ferns and mosses. The cheek rocks must be set so that their
bottoms are kept below the step treads. *Japanese garden,
Westchester County, New York*

CHAPTER TWO

INSPIRATIONS—LOOKING AT NATURE

Although forty years have passed since I first discovered Japanese gardens, I shall never forget their initial impact on me. I had entered a mystical landscape of dreams. The gardens' secluding screens of tile-topped earthen walls, bamboo fences and clipped hedges formed for me no barriers at all as I traveled far beyond their narrow precincts. I was transported out into the world over vast and varied landscapes of nature. Soaring and hovering like an eagle, I passed over gentle hills and stony peaks, dark valleys and craggy precipices, lofty waterfalls and gushing mountain brooks. And then, having gone beyond a rocky coast, I drifted like a petrel over archipelagoes of granitic islands, whose steep flanks formed coves and promontories washed by concentric swells rolling in from the farthest reaches of a boundless sea.

Those were adventures modulated in a thousand different ways upon each garden visit. But one garden in particular so touched me with its odd yet instant appeal, that the memory of my first contact returns as poignantly as if it were yesterday.

* * *

It is morning in Kyoto. Dawn has just broken over Higashiyama, the sacred, temple-studded mountains. I am standing with my bicycle by the entry gate in the wall that surrounds my house. It is perched on the west bank of the Kamo River, just upstream from the bridge of the Northern Imperial Shrine. I have only recently come to live in this former capital, which is over a thousand years old and is replete with moldering temples, palaces and mossy gardens. Now, slightly shivering in the morning chill of early May, I quietly close the gate behind me and pedal off to join my teacher, Tansai Sano. Today he will introduce me to Ryōanji, the Zen temple, and its garden of fifteen rocks.

This morning *sensei* will put me to a test: "Today you will get a shock," he has promised. "Ryōanji is unique. It works its own special magic. Take your time. There is no hurry." Looking puzzled, I nod, knowing that patience is my best response. I have no other choice.

Sano-sensei rides ahead as we make our way through narrow lanes, past flooded paddies waiting to receive the young rice plants that are still slender seedlings in propagation beds. To the accompaniment of the morning songs of cuckoos and nightingales we pass through forests of towering cryptomerias, cedars and pines. After one hour, we skirt a pond and finally

The mountains of Higashiyama. A temple is visible on Mount Hie, the
mountain in the background. *Higashiyama, Kyoto*

turn onto a dirt bypath. It is bounded on one side by a high hedgerow of bamboo and on the other by an ancient stucco wall, patchy with lichens and mold and capped by silvery gray tiles. On the other side of the wall lies Ryōanji.

Already the monks have been up for several hours. From within the temple yard comes the slow, rhythmic bong of the great bronze bell, then a dying, plangent tone followed by another bong. These punctuate the hum of sutra recitation by the monks and commentary by the abbot. Having reached the entrance, *sensei* pulls a bronze knob that projects through a hole in a low, narrow wooden door. A bell jingles on the other side of the wall, and soon there sounds the hollow clop-clop of a pair of *geta* on the stone pavement. A young shaven-headed acolyte opens the door and bows. He is wearing a faded blue cotton robe hitched up above his knees by a thin cord. In one hand he holds a broom of bamboo twigs which he has been using to gently sweep leaves from the moss groundcovers. He recognizes Sano-sensei from previous visits and bows. We bow in return to the young monk. He then ushers us over a steppingstone path skirting an outer court and leads the way through several doors and dark corridors. At last, we enter the abbot's chamber in the main temple pavilion, and crossing its dim, cavernous hall, we reach the great veranda facing the garden. From that raised position we gaze down upon a dazzling scene.

Before us stretches a barren, gravel-covered plain, roughly thirty by seventy feet. Straight, shallow furrows, raked six inches apart, run lengthwise back and forth over the rectangular plot. Two sides are bounded by a low wall of ochre, dun-streaked stucco. A low wing of the building and the veranda complete the enclosure. The flat sweep of the garden's surface is broken by fifteen undistinguished gray, weathered granite rocks, asymmetrically arranged in twos, threes and one group of five. Some of the rocks jut up like mountain peaks; others, set lower, recline on their backs or bellies. But upright or recumbent, they complement each other in some precise inner harmony, belonging there as if rooted forever in that seemingly limitless waste. They are like icebergs floating in Arctic waters, one-eighth above the surface and seven-eighths below.

An irregular belt of green moss surrounds each group of rocks, here, invading the coarse off-white grits in a dynamic salient as if it were a spit of land pushing seaward, and there, running back into a narrow band to form a shallow cove. Following the undulating contours of the sometimes convex, sometimes concave, girdles of moss, the gravel has been raked into sinuously curving concentric furrows that could be white, foamy rollers of surf breaking on some far-off island shore.

In that treeless garden, the only living element is the humble moss, wet and sparkling with morning dew. No swaying branch or fluttering leaf betrays the presence of even the faintest puff of an intruding breeze that might disturb the stillness, the static quality of the scene. Here nature seems to be holding her breath.

For a time I sit there, unmoving, silent. Minutes seem like hours. I turn to *sensei*, who has stepped back from the edge of the veranda. In my wonder and perplexity, I hold out both hands as if imploring him to provide a key to the scene spread out before me. With an enigmatic smile and a shrug of his shoulders, he responds: "Some say the rocks are a mother tiger playing with her cubs. Others, that it is just a miniature landscape of islands set in the Inland Sea. There are also art critics who say it can be appreciated merely as a carefully planned study in asymmetrical composition. And skeptics say it is all a funny joke, a clever trick devised by its designer, possibly either Sōami, the "Leonardo" of fifteenth-century Japan; Tokuhō Zenketsu, head priest at that time; or a collaboration of artists and priests." *Sensei's* voice trails off into silence. For a moment it is as if he is pondering how to answer my question. Then, in a more offhand tone, he continues: "In any case, I am sure it teased and confounded the monks, as well as the samurai and daimyo who would visit the temple whenever the world outside became more than they could bear. Who knows? Let each man believe what suits him best." *Sensei's* perceptive gaze now shifts from the garden to me. "But what does it mean to you?" he asks.

I have no answer, for in my naiveté and confusion, I fear lest I give my teacher the wrong answer. He understands and, in a gentler, less insistent tone, says: "Stay here a while; it is still early. Quietly look at the garden. Follow wherever it may lead you. Soon you may be out there above those distant islands. It may even take you beyond these old walls." Then he goes away. He knows I have to make the journey alone.

* * *

As the years went by, I would ask myself again and again what it was that day that made the garden in Ryōanji so unique. Why had my sense of scale been distorted? What was it that gave it such power? More than simply the beauty of the weathered granite surfaces, wasn't it also their disposition, their artful arrangement? The maker obviously was a keen and constant observer of landscapes in the wild, someone who had traveled, seen the world with knowing eyes and, with an analytical mind, had studied both the micro and the macro in nature. Did it also have something to do with man's sense of his place in the world, the universe? With the terrestrial level as contrasted with the heavenly? What primordial glimmerings were stirred?

Later, I found that, despite the great differences in the social structures, histories and traditions of China and Japan, Chinese gardens, too, allude to magic and mystery, achieving a comparable power to transport the observer beyond the limiting walls of his garden and into the wide world beyond.

The questions raised here may arise in the mind of anyone who has felt the captivating power of the rockery of Oriental gardens. My aim here is to develop an understanding of the process of rock arrangement, to inspire, and to instill confidence in the garden lover to create with rocks another vast and evocative world on his own patch of earth.

My involvement started early in life. I began looking at each natural landscape with questioning eyes trying to understand how the scene was put together, how each feature related to the other parts of the landscape. It all seemed so simple, so artless, yet so perfect. Although each

The essence of this Zen temple garden is succinctly expressed by the poet Lindley W. Hubbell in this poem, "The Rock Garden at Ryōanji."

This is the ultimate subtlety of art,
The marrow in the bones:
A rectangle of raked gravel
And a few stones.

Laid out at the end of the fifteenth century, the garden is about the size of a tennis court and was made to be viewed only from the veranda of the temple's main hall. The flat rectangle of raked gravel contains five groups of rocks—fifteen in all—arranged successively in groups of five, two, three, two and three. In the overall composition there seems to be a perfect occult balance between groups. Equilibrium also exists within each group of rocks. In their simple forms, the rocks themselves are unexceptional, but the complex abstraction of their arrangement, a series of interwoven triangles, is what brings a powerful impact to the scene. Of course, it is not only the rocks, but the space and sense of motion created. There is both emptiness and fullness. *Ryōanji, Kyoto*

25

Are we gazing down on cliffs rising precipitously hundreds of feet below, or looking at a rocky shoreline only a few feet away? *Moosehead Lake, Maine*

Are they uninhabited landscapes of bare, stony hills amid arid desert basins at the edge of a barren sea, as viewed from an airplane flying 20,000 feet above? Are they expertly constructed models of a landscape for a museum diorama? Or are they something else? Perfect examples of rockery that cause the scale to oscillate in the viewer's mind. Is he five feet away or miles above? Garden builders working with rocks can learn a lot from pondering these scenes. *Oregon Coast*

landscape was different, one could find likenesses—analogies, but never true copies. Even then, I learned that nature does not duplicate without introducing differences of some sort. Neither in animals nor in plants or such inanimate things as rocks are there two exactly the same. That recognition made even more exciting the discovery of something new in each encounter.

I remember when I was eight, feeling the ups and downs of the land with delight while on a Sunday drive with my father through the countryside of rural New Jersey, the Catskill Mountains of New York State, and the Litchfield Hills of Connecticut. As the road rose and fell with the surrounding landscape of mountains, hills and valleys, I had the sensation of bonding intimately with it. Years later, traveling in China's Sichuan Province, that early childhood memory came back to me. This time, however, I felt I had entered one of those enchanting handscrolls by an early Qing painter, depicting in ink and color a splendid procession of the Kangxi emperor through grand landscapes of the Celestial Middle Kingdom. The artist's representation of towering cliffs, narrow mountain passes and deep declivities were far from realistic, yet so aptly drawn that one felt in every way a participant, totally immersed in the enfolding scenes.

But long before I set eyes upon China, Japan became my introduction to Asia. In 1950 I lived in a house perched high up on a green hillside in old Kamakura. To reach the house I would first take a country road that threaded its way between paddy fields before climbing through terraced uplands, then squeezing into a perpetually

dark defile formed by high rock walls, and at last emerging onto a sunny plateau. The contrast between that final gloomy passage and the bright landscape that lay ahead seemed always to whet my expectation of viewing Mount Fuji, towering above its base of lesser peaks off in the distance. Named by the local folks "O-Yama" (Honorable Mountain), Mount Fuji exerted a unifying force upon those who lived within sight of its mass. At first, I was a stranger in that little world at the western reaches of the broad, teeming Kanto Plain. But that hovering immanence, always on the horizon and still regarded as sacred, gave neighbors a shared experience to talk about. Though we led very different lives, we had the same view from our houses.

It was that sleeping volcano that first brought me in touch with Dr. Saito, a

Agglomerations of *taihu* limestone rocks introduce an element of fantasy into gardens. These rock formations suggest a magical landscape of cliffs and crags on intricately eroded bases. *Canglangting, Suzhou, China*

country physician and neighbor who became a valued friend. Mornings I used to meet him on the road, carrying his black medical bag. We smiled and bowed, and I, at first self-consciously, would greet him: "*Ohaiyō-gozaimasu, Saito-sensei* (Good morning, Dr. Saito)." He points to Mount Fuji, fifty miles away. Its symmetrical peak is thrusting through a belt of streaming clouds which enshrouds its upper slopes. "O-Yama is showing her face today," he says with a smile. Then he passes on, trudging up the road on his daily rounds.

In all seasons the mountain was a subject of conversation. In the summer Dr. Saito would remark that the color of the bare cinders of once molten lava now looked a rich purple. From October through May we marveled how the snow-capped heights had become a great white cone, hardly distinguishable from its encircling ring of clouds.

Several times Dr. Saito invited me to see his garden. My first glimpse showed him to be a close observer of the natural landscape. In the small space of his garden, through sensitive molding of its topography and arrangement of the rocks, he unmistakably had evoked a wider world. Even Mount Fuji was suggested there, he said, to make up for days when clouds hid the distant mountain from view.

The type of person who feels such a profound affinity with the features of a natural landscape observes more extensively those myriad examples around him. This can be done simply by devoting attention to the environment while going about daily activities, ranging from stopping to look at an excavation, to noting the landscape passing beneath while riding in an airplane as it flies cross-country.

For example, what inspiration will I get if I head west from the East Coast of the United States? What land forms will I encounter? First, the receding ranges of wooded Appalachian hills separated by green valleys formed by rivers and streams that have cut their courses through these uplands. In some places, they have formed deep defiles between narrow ridges; in others, more ancient terrain worn down into broad valleys of cultivated agricultural fields interspersed with slower moving, meandering streams. From the air are revealed the oxbow arcs and curves of the now dry beds of ancient water courses.

Passing over the Great Plains, with their seemingly endless stretches of prairie farms dotted with woodlots and connected by roads that lead on and on to distant horizons, I look down into the basins of the Mississippi and Missouri rivers, the great waterways that drain America's midsection. As the rivers twist and turn, I notice how they eat away at their concave banks and deposit rocks, gravel, sand and silt on their convex banks.

Then, leaving the flatlands, I encounter the ranges of the Rocky Mountains looming up ahead. I tell myself: Observe the outline of their profiles, the particular patterns made at their intersections, and note how the successive ranges appear lighter in tone as they recede into the distance. Observe, too, the forms of mountain peaks and how they mask each other so that they appear to be constantly shifting as I move past them. See how light strikes these mountaintops, and note the effect of shadows formed by one peak as it masks its neighbor. Notice the changes in the effect of shifting light and shadow as the day moves from morning to late afternoon—what a rocky pinnacle looks like at noon as compared with the light of early morning and late afternoon.

In winter, I observe the pattern of snow on the high ranges and peaks: where it is pocketed and where, on south-facing slopes, it has melted or blown away. Look at the effect created by trees masking the view of parts of the rocky areas, and compare the moist, green hills and mountains with an arid desert landscape where plant life is sparse and where the brown, ochre and red rocks on slopes and hilltops

Mount Fuji

Mature rice growing in paddies along the shoreside road to Enoshima. *Katase, Kanagawa Prefecture*

appear more dominant and harsher.

See how a particular species of plants grows around rock formations at different elevations, and how some species seem to thrive under adverse conditions in rocky environments. Deprived of plentiful water and buffeted by strong winds, but with their roots penetrating into the crevices and cracks of their stony footholds, they defy the harshest punishment to survive. I feel respect and admiration for these plants upon seeing the evidence of their tenacity. Their battle for survival is a lesson taught

High plains and distant mountain ranges. *Taos, New Mexico*

in nature's wild landscape, one that can inspire the creator of rock compositions in a garden. I have seen such examples in a wide variety of landscapes: the rock-bound coast of Maine and lofty cliffs of New York State; the deserts of Arizona and New Mexico; the coasts of California and Oregon; and even the rocky islets in Japan's Inland Sea.

Still heading westward and having

Rice terraces: the product of a thousand years of care
and cultivation. *Near Ubud, Bali, Indonesia*

Above and below: A deep valley and rugged cliffs. *New Mexico*

passed over the Rocky Mountains and the deserts, the West Coast lies before me. I observe how bluffs emerge ,from the sea and see the action of waves breaking against them to form promontories separated by bays and coves. I note how sandy beaches are formed in coves as water erodes the cliffs of headlands, and how it carries the detritus to make sand spits appear. And venturing inland to the Cascades, I see how some mountain peaks look so symmetrical and settled. Some of the symmetry is formed by volcanoes, while other mountains appear almost unbalanced and precarious. Similarly, rock formations in gardens may also seem static or dynamic.

I pay attention, too, to the different forms of waterfalls, cascades and rapids: how some falls are broad, mighty and thunderous; others, discrete ribbons of water or thin trickles and sprays.

By ranging over the natural landscape, whether in his own country or in some far-off land, the creator of evocative garden landscapes can build up in his mind a reservoir, a treasury of images that can be dredged up from the depths of his memory. This reservoir will be the source of inspiration and guidance in his work with gardens, and with rocks in particular. Does he want to evoke a vision of gentle hills, a stony stream bed, a waterfall, a rocky shoreline, a range of distant mountains, or towering peaks at near range? All such features can be created in a garden when the designer-creator has drawn upon the palette of natural sights in his memory.

Taihu rocks in a Chinese garden evoke myriad images,
forever stimulating the imagination. *Gardens in Suzhou,
China*

CHAPTER THREE

CHINA AND JAPAN—HISTORIES AND CONTRASTS

A PAIR OF STONES

Two chunks of gray-green stone,
their shapes grotesque and unsightly,
wholly unfit for practical uses —
ordinary people despise them, leave them untouched.
Formed in the time of primal chaos,
they took their place at the mouth of Lake Taihu,
ten thousand ages resting by the lakeshore,
in one morning coming into my hands!

Pole-bearers have brought them to my prefectural office
where I wash and scrub away mud and stains.
The hollows are black, deeply scarred in mist,
crevices green with the rich hue of moss.
Aged dragons coiled to form their feet,
old swords stuck in for the crown,
I suddenly wonder if they didn't plummet from Heaven,
so different from anything in this human realm!

One will do to prop up my lute,
one to be a reservoir for my wine.
The tip of one shoots up several yards,
the other has a hollow, will hold a gallon of liquid!
My five-stringed instrument leaning on the left one,
my single wine cup set on the right,
I'll dip from the hollowed cask and it will never go dry,
though drunkenness long since has toppled me over.

Every person has something he loves,
and things all yearn for a companion.
More and more I fear that gatherings of the young
no longer will welcome a white-haired gentleman.
I turn my head, ask this pair of stones
if they'd consent to keep an old man company.
And though the stones are powerless to speak,
they agree that we three should be friends.

—*Bai Juyi [Po Chü-i] (772–846)*

A waterfall in two tiers. Water is pumped to the fall's upper basin as it is recirculated out of the pond, which is a gunnite shell. The individual rocks in the water impart an illusion of distance and vanishing perspective for viewers around the pond's edges. *Park Garden Building, Fountainhead Corporate Park, Tempe, Arizona*

Granite rock outcroppings along a mountain path—sources of both inspiration and supply for landscape architects, garden builders, and artists. *Tianpingshan, Jiangsu, China*

In reply to Emperor Gao's inquiry:
"Among the hills, what have you?"

Among the hills, what have I?
On the ridges there are many white clouds;
But these are only for my own enjoyment —
They cannot be caught and sent on to your Majesty.
—*Tao Hongjing (452–536)*

———

Question and Answer among the Mountains

You ask me why I dwell in the green mountain;
I smile and make no reply for my heart is free of care.
As the peach blossom flows down stream and is gone into
the unknown,
I have a world apart that is not among men.
—*Li Bo (701–762)*

———

On the Road to Nara

Oh, these spring days!
A nameless little mountain,
wrapped in morning haze!
—*Matsuo Bashō (1644–1694)*

On the Mountain Pass

Here on the mountain pass,
somehow they draw one's heart so —
   violets in the grass.
      —*Matsuo Bashō (1644–1694)*

——

The Little Valley in Spring

A mountain stream:
even the stones make songs —
   wild cherry trees.
      —*Onitsura (1660–1738)*

——

Magnificent Peak

By its own nature it towers above the tangle of
rivers.
Don't say it's a lot of dirt piled high.
Without end the mist of dawn, the evening cloud draw
their shadows across it.
From the four directions you can look up and see it
green and steep and wild.
      —*Musō Soseki (1275–1351)*

A shallow stream flowing over a stony bed between massive rocks suggests a river of rapids within a deep gorge. The side rocks force the water to flow in an irregular course, hiding its source and destination. *Ryōanji, Kyoto*

The first three poems reflect the deep veneration of nature inspired by Taoism in the Chinese. Composed centuries later in Japan, the three *haiku* and one poem in that unique, spare expression of human emotion also show an intense awareness towards objects of nature. These poems all convey the poets' similar feelings on encountering the raw landscapes of nature, particularly the impact upon them of mountain scenes.

In both China and Japan, this yearning for those uncultivated, pristine heights inevitably led to the making of gardens that would evoke this feeling. In both lands, while human life was perceived as brief, it was nature that was seen to endure.

Although gardens in Japan at first shared features with those of Tang China, they ultimately went in a different direction. Such divergence was of course inevitable, for despite the strong influences upon Japan of all aspects of Chinese esthetic, intellectual and religious experience—writing, dress, art, architecture, cuisine, Taoism—immutable differences existed between the two countries. Climate, geography, ethnic composition, history and social organization, for example, were so different that they were bound to affect the two countries' views of the world. Those differences carried over into all aspects of the lives of the Japanese and Chinese, dividing the two peoples too deeply and fundamentally to permit them to continue down the same path.

The most obvious disparity was their respective locations on the globe. Both were at the eastern edge of Asia and therefore isolated from the rest of the world, especially from the other burgeoning centers of civilization in Europe and the Middle East. Yet China, though surrounded on its northern and western approaches by vast deserts and plains, still had periodic commercial contacts with those cultures of Europe, India and the Middle East.

Japan, on the other hand, remained insular in its thinking and isolated from frequent and easy contact with the rest of the world. Surrounded by water, it was more easily defensible and, unlike China, did not have to contend with barbarian invaders sweeping down from the north across the steppes of Mongolia. It never had to spend its treasure on a "Great Wall." Invasion from the sea, though possible and once attempted unsuccessfully by a Mongol emperor, was never a constant threat or concern. The only "invasion" was a cultural one from Korea and China, and it, in fact, was welcomed.

Global location also influences climate. China, with its continental weather system, was much more subject to extremes of cold and heat, drought and flood, while Japan's moderate marine climate protected it from such problems. Rainfall was usually sufficient to provide enough water for Japan's paddy rice agriculture.

The geographies of the two countries were another powerful factor that made for differences. Most obvious is the disparity in their sizes. China is among the six largest countries in the world, with a constantly growing population. Japan, a nation of four main islands with a smaller population and only meager natural resources, could not match China's power.

Geologically, China has undergone millions of years of epochal metamorphosis, its

In a Chinese garden courtyard, the weight of architecture is deftly counterbalanced by imposing rocks set upright in prominent positions. They compete with the man-made structures, while evoking memories of distant mountain landscapes. *Suzhou, China*

Conveying an impression of mountains and highlands, this rock acts as a strong element to counterbalance the effect of the plantings. *Ryōanji, Kyoto*

Karst-eroded limestone topography: inspiration for
landscape architects, garden builders and painters.
Li River, Guilin, China

vast territory first rising then falling. Mountains were formed, then worn down into broad plains and deltas. Sometimes they were covered by great shallow seas, which later disappeared as the land rose again to become high hills and mountains. Thus, a complex geology was formed of granites, basalts, limestone and a variety of minerals.

Japan, a land geologically younger than China, was formed mainly by volcanism. Indeed, it still contains a number of active volcanoes and is racked by frequent earthquakes. Unlike China, Japan has not been shaped to any great extent by the erosive forces of wind and water. Japan's rock resources are mainly igneous in origin—metamorphosed rock, granites, basalts and cherts, with sedimentary rock to a much lesser degree.

Because of their dissimilar geological histories, the topographies of the two countries look quite different. China has great plains, deserts, the Himalaya and Tianshan ranges, broad river valleys and wide alluvial deltas. Japan, on the other hand, except for the extensive Kanto and Kansai plains and smaller coastal flatlands, is mainly covered with mountains and hills, interspersed with narrow valleys. And since the mountains are close to the coast, the rivers are too shallow to be navigable, unlike China's great rivers: the Yangtze, Yellow, Pearl, Li and others. As a result, Japan could never depend upon a network of navigable rivers and canals for internal transportation and communication. Its regions, villages and towns were much more isolated from each other, which, in turn, favored less centralized governmental control, with a resultant feudalism

persisting in one form or another up to modern times.

Thus, over the course of centuries, the physical environment of the two countries came to shape their cultures and histories. Despite dynastic changes, China's mandarin government fostered a static society with long periods of calm, while Japan, divided into feudal fiefdoms, was for centuries the scene of instability and civil wars. The only way to achieve preeminence was by fighting one's way to the top. The emperor, reigning in name only, was merely the figurehead for a series of military dictators who, in shifting alliances with powerful daimyo feudal lords and their samurai warriors, ruled the country. Unlike China, there was no such thing as a centralized bureaucracy of mandarins who gained access to power through regular examinations. In China, power came through academic success; in Japan, through military success.

Nevertheless, civil affairs and culture in both countries were tempered by the influence of the cults of Taoism and Confucianism, and the religion of Buddhism.

Taoism, that appealing and romantic philosophic system of Chinese thought, pervaded Chinese and Japanese life and art. Propounded and elucidated from the sixth century B.C. onward first by Laozi, then Zhuangzi, Taoism signaled escape from the artificiality of a worldly life, the throwing off of the stifling constraints of Confucian precepts, and a return to nature, primitivism and the rural ideal.

In his book *Taoism: The Road to Immortality*, John Blofeld fluently and elegantly explains the effects of Taoism upon

Chinese and Japanese culture.

Again and again Laozi emphasizes the unwisdom of seeking prominence, wealth or status; the wisdom of being simple and artless—hence that graphic image, the uncarved block. This image perfectly accords with what is meant by 'becoming an immortal' and underlies much of Japanese as well as Chinese art and culture. In the Far East, restraint and simplicity have long been regarded as the hallmark of true greatness, and this principle is inherent in the best of the poetry and visual arts of China and Japan, where the loveliest poems consist of a few bare syllables; the finest paintings are often executed with an astonishing economy of brush-strokes and with no color but the various shades of watered black ink on a white surface; the most exquisite ceramics are notable for extreme simplicity; and the most elegant furniture owes almost the whole of its beauty to simplicity of line.

This love of the simple and unassuming derives from intuitive perception of the nature of the Tao. Formless and void, the Tao is the source of all the myriad forms. Mother of the universe and sustainer of all creatures, it is perfectly indifferent to—indeed unconscious of its bounty. Effortlessly it replenishes lack and diminishes excess, accomplishing all that is required without forethought, strain or hurry. It is at once both void and form, the one aspect being essential to the other, just as voidness is essential to a vessel, unimpeded space to a window or door.

This teaching contributed to the fondness of Taoist adepts for the solitude of the mountains where one can be free to act in accordance with the prompting of the heart, unfettered by laws or usages of society.

Fondness for mountains, trees, streams, pools and flowers is, of course, not limited to the Chinese; other peoples also have recognized them as the abodes of gods and spirits, but some manifestations of this fondness are peculiarly Chinese [and also Japanese: author's interpellation]. *Take, for example, the extraordinary reverence for rocks, which certainly arose from a quality in stone that graphically suggests the interchangeability of all of the myriad objects created by the* Tao. *It is rare to find a mountain ridge or rocky eminence of any sort that has not been likened to something alive.*

The insistence of Laozi and Chuangzi [Zhuangzi] *on spiritual withdrawal from the world doubtless contributed to the notion of actual physical withdrawal. The Taoist True Man, unlike his Confucian counterpart, had no desire to involve himself in the task of reforming society; and it was obvious that the conquest of desire could be carried out more easily in the solitude of the mountains than in densely populated towns and villages. Taoists bent on cultivating the Way usually did inhabit solitary places. Indeed, the Chinese ideogram for 'immortal' also bears the connotation 'mountain man', being a combination of the radical for man and the radical for mountain. From an early date the Taoist ideal was of a sage who, besides being inspired with intuitive understanding of the Way, loved to wander alone among majestic peaks, with the sun and moon for lamps, the sky for his roof and the softly waving grasses for a bed.*

In contrast to Taoism, Confucius and his later followers gave China a system of ethics and conduct which formed the basis of the Chinese social structure—a hierarchy based on obedience to authority, from the authority of the head of the household up to that of the emperor. Taoism, on the other hand, encouraged a sense of individualism, enjoyment of life and nature, yet with respect for their mysteries and superstitions.

Buddhism was introduced into Japan from China by way of Korea in the sixth century and added a layer of moral teaching

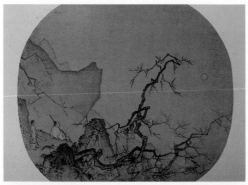

Painting of a Taoist scholar contemplating the moon in a mountain retreat, surrounded by stony crags. *Ma Yuan, 12–13th century, (Southern Song)*

This sixteenth-century Zen garden in a space only nine feet wide transports the beholder far away to distant mountains and ranges of hills, valleys, a waterfall and a river. The power of its symbolism stems from the forms of the rocks themselves and from the perfect juxtaposition of their vertical and horizontal forms against the misty backdrop of the white plaster walls. Its design is attributed to Sōami, the landscape painter. *Daisen-in, Daitokuji, Kyoto*

The large rocks' rugged forms suggest high mountains jutting up from the lower foothills of the sheared azaleas. Though the rocks and shrubs are strong statements, their weight is balanced by the wide expanse of the gravel "sea" of *hakusha* in this temple garden. *Kyoto*

and concern for the soul. But in the twelfth century, with the arrival from China of the Zen sect of Buddhism (termed "Chan" in Chinese), a more anti-scholastic, intuitive strain entered into Japanese religious life. Thomas Hoover describes early Chan as deriving some of its philosophical basis from Taoist ideas in China, with its light-hearted irreverence and love of nature: *Whether Chinese Zen was really Buddhism masquerading as Taoism, or Taoism disguised as Buddhism has never been fully established—it contains elements of both.*

In Japan, Zen had a strong influence on the arts, especially poetry, painting and garden design. Zen priest garden builders introduced abstract landscapes—such as those at Kyoto's Daitokuji and Ryōanji—into their naturalistic compositions of rock.

The totality of Taoism, Confucianism and Buddhism, together with all the elements of China's more advanced culture, appealed to the Japanese. Up to that time, Japan's spiritual life had consisted of Shinto, a pervasive animism involving fertility cults and recognition of an indwelling spirit world within many elements of nature—streams, trees, mountains, seas, rocks. The ethical and religious systems from China introduced more complex concepts of social structure, duty, ethics, morality and concern for the afterlife, concepts which appealed to the Japanese mind that hungered for a more profound and sophisticated world view.

Along with the much-admired and eagerly adopted social and religious concepts, changes also flowered in the arts: painting, sculpture, architecture and literature. These soon developed a native style, uniquely Japanese, that became a reflection of the differences between the two cultures. Such differences may be seen by comparing, for example, a finely potted Song porcelain *longchuan* bowl with the rougher forms and textures of a *shigaraki* bowl used in *cha-no-yu* (the tea ceremony). While the Chinese appreciate refined, pristine elegance, the Japanese are more preoccupied with chance, nature's spontaneity, and the weathering of time, as expressed by the concepts of *shibusa, sabi, wabi* and *yūgen*. (Although there is a labored precision in these, too, it is deliberately hidden.) Such differences are carried over into the other arts of poetry, painting, architecture and garden design.

In China, man-made landscapes had a much more mundane basis than those of Japan—simply imperial power. Pleasure gardens were first built for the emperor and his court. Designed on a grand scale and covering hundreds of acres, they encompassed hills and woods filled with flowering trees and shrubs, streams, ponds and lakes, and were used for outings and hunting parties. In later periods, lesser court officials and wealthy merchants had their own estates: family compounds with opulent gardens, all on land reduced in scale from that of the imperial court. This reduction in size forced garden builders to design topography and features which conveyed the impression that one had entered a much vaster natural landscape.

The organization of the Chinese family system, in which several generations of relations lived within one compound, required a design that allowed privacy, while at the same time facilitating convenient interaction between all its members. Thus, grandparents, parents and children

Above: A courtyard garden. The rock work's irregular profile is echoed by the undulating masonry wall which appears to recede and almost disappear into the background foliage. *Zhuozhengyuan, Suzhou, China*

Center and below: The *taihu* rocks of Chinese gardens, in their convoluted surfaces and pierced branching, seem to be forever evolving: they may suggest an island, a hill, a craggy peak, a waterfall, or even animals and human beings. *Gardens in Suzhou, China*

Above: A subsidiary garden path in a temple grounds. No border slabs define the path, and consequently no overpowering formality exists. This looseness is furthered by combining cut stone pieces with much smaller natural stones set with wide joints. *Ryōanji, Kyoto*

Below: The weight of the *chōzubachi* high water basin is nicely counterbalanced by the "mountain" boulder, which, in turn, is visually supported by the recumbent rock. The placement of those three stone objects illustrates again adherence to the principle of the *sanzon* triad. *Ginkakuji, Kyoto*

of one branch of the extended family would have their own house and private courtyard within the larger garden landscape. Yet this would be connected by covered walkways, bridges and paths to the houses of aunts, uncles and cousins living in similar arrangements in other sections of the garden compound. The landscape separating the individual houses and courtyards was designed to incorporate natural features such as streams, hills, ponds, and was planted with copses of trees, shrubs and flower beds. These were all interspersed with small structures, such as a trellis here, and there, a *ting* (pavilion) and *lang* (covered walkway). Throughout the garden were strewn arrangements of rockery, mostly the fantastic, lacy limestone *taihu* rock.

The classical Chinese garden, as exemplified by those that survive today, is a reflection of the values and tastes of Chinese upper-class society of the Ming and Qing dynasties. Its extensive grounds demonstrated the cohesiveness of the family system, while the high masonry walls surrounding the compound provided protection and privacy from the outside world. Ornate, colorful architecture showed the taste and materialistic values of the owner, as did walled-in private courtyards paved in geometric brick and stone mosaic patterns, and plantings with free-standing *taihu* rocks. The enclosed courtyards served as extensions of each house's living space, but there were always gates or doors in the wall, opening up into the larger, more naturalistic communal landscape that served both as a buffer zone against and an avenue of communication to the other branches of

An entryway garden for a Zen temple, consisting of sparse evergreen
plantings under the sheltering branch of a Japanese red pine. The two
rocks—one dominant, the other, subsidiary—add the necessary element
of earth, the *yin-yang* duality, to balance out the weight of the plantings.
The late February snowfall creates a rhythmic pattern on the wall's tile
coping. The path's granite slab pavers add a minor note of order. All in
all, there is a pervasive sense of restraint, quietness and understatement.
Zuihō-in, Daitokuji, Kyoto

The garden is situated at the foot of a steep hillside which gathers a lot of water run-off during heavy rains. Hence the need for large rocks set close together and overlapping as they follow the irregular winding outline of the narrow pond. In storms, the pond can momentarily become a swiftly flowing stream. Broadleaved evergreen trees and shrubs, together with ferns and mosses, thrive in the damp shade. *Fuyō-en, Sakamoto, Shiga Prefecture*

the family. A vivid description of these arrangements can be found in the novel *Story of the Stone* (or *Dream of the Red Chamber*) by Cao Xueqin. All in all, the Chinese garden was a substantial creation: heavy, ponderous, imposing and symbolic of power—both financial and political. It survived the changes in society caused by dynastic wars right up until 1949, when the Communist revolution swept away that unique family system. The walled family compounds with their gardens and buildings were expropriated by the state. Today they are open to the public and are maintained by the local municipalities.

Compared to the classical Chinese garden, the Japanese garden presents a more moderate, less imposing face. Though extensive stroll gardens, built for the imperial family and the daimyo lords, were initially patterned after examples from Tang China (see the description of Prince Genji's garden in Lady Murasaki Shikibu's eleventh-century novel *Tale of Genji*), later gardens were much more restrained in scale and taste. In Japan, appreciation of and desire for gardens descended to a much broader population base than in China, particularly with the rise of the merchant class during the years of the Tokugawa Shogunate (1600–1868). And, aside from large stroll gardens built for the wealthy, gardens were constructed on a much smaller scale. They were designed to be viewed from certain vantage points—either from the veranda of the house or from points along a pathway. They were not meant to be physically occupied, unlike Chinese gardens.

Visually, though, the garden space did become part of the living space of the

The heavy, single-spanned stone bridge expresses the power of the Shogunate. The bridge abutments of massive stone blocks are similar to the stone of the castle's wall fortifications. No attempt was made to introduce natural stone into the abutments, almost as if it were demonstrating that the Shogun's power rested on his own efforts rather than on nature. *Nijō Castle, Kyoto*

Granite boulders, in two groups of five each, form a balanced composition while, at the same time, providing the foil of a substantial rock mass heavy enough to offset the mass of tree and shrubs along the pathway—an example of the duality of *yin-yang*. *Kinkakuji, Kyoto*

Above: Rocks suggesting a rugged, high peak with lower cliffs. The smaller rocks in front give a sense of support and stability while breaking up the space between the viewer and the background, thereby creating the impression of greater distance from the viewer.
Taizō-in, Myōshinji, Kyoto

Below: The irregular rocky shoreline of a clay-lined pond. Promontories are accentuated with large rocks, while the recessed coves are formed with smaller rocks. *Kinkakuji, Kyoto*

house. When the *shōji* panels were slid open, the garden seemed to become an extension of the house, and thus a part of the viewer's world. This world was separated from the outside, not by ten-foot high, whitewashed masonry walls as in China, but by low, dun-colored or white tile-capped walls, bamboo fences, or simply by clipped evergreen hedges. It is almost as if the enclosures were meant to keep the viewer within from being disturbed by the sight of extraneous elements. These boundaries offered not physical protection from the outside world, but freedom from the psychological or visual disturbance this world might cause.

In contrast to the Chinese predilection for ornate and complex architectural forms, the architecture in Japanese gardens is simple: sometimes refined, sometimes rustic. There are no mosaic–paved courtyards, but rather, groundcovers of moss and lawn; paths of gravel; natural or cut stone slab steppingstones; or *nobedan* (stone carpet) panels of natural and cut stone set in a matrix of mortar, sand or clay. Often, in place of the actual ponds and streams in Chinese gardens, the Japanese resorted to using groundcovers of *shirakawazuna*, fine off-white gravel of decomposed rotten granite, which they raked into swirls and wave patterns to simulate water. Trying to "see" water in the dry gravel terrain appealed to the Japanese fascination with abstraction.

In the Japanese garden there has always been both a sense of the passing of time and a feeling of time stood still. This might seem paradoxical and contradictory but, to the Japanese mind, it is perfectly natural, for time, like music, has a variety

Despite the rock's massive upper section that is tenuously connected to the earth, balanced, it seems to be defying gravity as if it were a balloon tugging at its moorings, straining to fly off into the blue. *Wangshiyuan, Suzhou, China*

A *karesansui* composition alongside a path suggests islands in the sea. There is occult balance in which the empty gravel-covered terrain counterbalances the rocks. The one larger rock placed in front acts as if it were a partially submerged reef of stone. With each in a position of repose, the rocks evoke an atmosphere of stability and calm. *Taizo-in, Myōshinji, Kyoto*

of tempos: *presto, andante* and *largo.* The feeling of the movement of time is conveyed by weathering, by the accumulation of lichens and moss on rocks and stone, and by the seasonal growth of plants. The static quality, on the other hand, is maintained by controlling such seasonal growth though regular and assiduous pruning, and by dependence upon slow growing evergreen trees and shrubs, both broadleaf and needled, as the basic structural plants in the garden.

But even more important in conveying this sense of permanence and stability in the Japanese garden is the choice of rocks. In contrast to the Chinese appetite for the seemingly malleable *taihu* limestone, the Japanese preference for granite illustrates important philosophic differences between their approaches to garden design.

Taihu rocks, with all their nooks and crannies, articulations and perforations, remain complex forms. Like soft clouds or frozen sea foam, they appear plastic and pliable: forever changing, floating, light and insubstantial. With their weird shapes and undulations, they convey an element of mystery and fantasy, at times even perplexing and sinister. But time has little effect on these rocks. In their pale gray shades they remain forever young, the Dorian Gray of the garden world.

Compare, then, these *taihu* rocks with the down-to-earth and apparently simple shapes and textures of rocks in a Japanese garden. Most sought after are the robust granites, igneous rocks that over eons have been metamorphosed into hard stone. Resistant to the forces of nature and time, they nevertheless show evidence of the passage of time with their accumulations of lichens and discoloration from weathering. Seemingly sprouting from the garden soil, yet firmly rooted in place, they represent to the Japanese mind anchors of stability and durability in a world where so much has been transitory—particularly the buildings of wood and paper. The

The sheared forms of the evergreen trees provide the right weight, uniformity and simplicity of texture as background for the complex arrangement of rocks. Such a rock grouping needs the plain wall of compact foliage as a backdrop; they would be lost in front of a backdrop of unsheared plantings. The dessicated, gnarled branch of the old cedar seems like a dragon writhing above its mountain lair. *Konchi-in, Nanzenji, Kyoto*

Buddhist consciousness and acceptance of the transiency of life only strengthens the Japanese desire for at least one small corner in their daily environment where they can have visual contact with familiar, enduring and consoling elements, such as that provided by even a few rocks placed in their gardens. Additionally, adherence to the precepts of Buddhism does not extinguish the belief in the indwelling spirits of rocks. How, the Japanese ask themselves, can a spirit live in a soft Chinese *taihu* rock perforated with so many holes? Surely, it is bound to slip away in such an insubstantial home.

Both the Chinese and the Japanese, however, want their rocks to suggest the greater mountain landscapes far removed from their home environments. The ability to represent vast size is therefore considered central to a rock's value. But while the Chinese believe that fantasy, magic and mystery—often represented in their garden rockery by stark monoliths—can help to evoke vast mountain scenes, the Japanese try to evoke the same mental pictures through using elemental granite forms. When arranged in artful compositions, simple abstractions symbolic of the larger landscape features of nature, they too work magic in the mind of the beholder.

To the Japanese mind, a garden is complete only when it contains rock as well as plants. Together, they represent the reality of the world, the concept of *yin* and *yang* which is the very essence of existence. *Yin*—rock—in transition to soil, represents the passive, receptive element (Mother Earth), while *yang*—plants—is the active, aggressive, growing element. They make up the female and male components of creation. Thus, the presence of both rock and plants in a garden is a step towards achieving the sense of completeness which relieves the garden of flimsiness, superficiality, or the sense that something is lacking.

CHAPTER FOUR

FUNCTIONS OF ROCKS IN A GARDEN

Rocks can function in myriad ways, standing alone or in combinations. Indeed, I would say that the more roles a rock can play at the same time, the more successful the design.

In purely utilitarian terms, rocks may be arranged as a free-standing wall to screen undesirable views from the garden; as a barrier to keep the outside world from intruding; as a fence to keep children and pets from straying; or as a neutral background against which other garden elements may be arranged.

Rocks may also be placed as a wall to retain a slope or terrace. In most instances, this may be achieved using large boulders to form a retaining wall even as high as six feet and at a considerably lower cost than a retaining wall of reinforced concrete or a wall laid by a stonemason in courses of smaller rocks.

Along streams, other bodies of water and road cuts, rocks can be used to build revetments. They can form waterfalls, cascades and rapids in streams. Or, they may be embedded in a stream bottom to serve as steppingstones that either bridge the stream or follow the water course, enabling a summer visitor to take advantage of the cooler air temperature directly above the water while keeping his feet dry.

Rocks may also be used to mark a change in direction of a path or roadway, as a diversionary blocking element, or along garden steps and ramps as cheek rocks, preventing soil along the sides from spilling back onto the steps.

Between a basically practical utilitarian function and a purely abstract decorative role, there is a middle ground where rocks serve as realistic or representational elements in a man-made landscape. This is most evident when the garden builder has decided to alter the landscape character radically. Where the land is level, he regrades the topography to form hills and mountains. Where there is only earth, he adds rocks to make peaks, cliffs and crags, and rocky ledges. Where there are featureless shorelines around a pond or lake, he places rocks to form rocky promontories, peninsulas, and off-shore islands. Thus, although the rocks themselves form a realistic, naturalistic composition, they can change the character of the landscape dramatically.

Having assiduously studied nature's features, the garden builder may attempt to replicate them in the garden. He is less concerned with symbolism and more with the creation of a landscape that requires little interpretation or imagination on the

To retain a high embankment above a pond, large rocks are required. They are set deeply into the earth and in some cases must be reinforced with a concrete base setting bed. The moss-covered hillside is terraced with swales to divert laterally much of the water run-off during downpours of rain. The diversionary swales also prevent mud and debris from washing into the pool. The lichens on the rocks imbue the scene with a feeling of age. *Ginkakuji, Kyoto*

part of the garden viewer. It is a style practiced outside of Japan and China. If done well it is pleasing to the eye, but it does not demand the same mental effort of the viewer as the Japanese and Chinese approach, which seeks also to inject symbolism into the scene.

Rocks may be used without any reference to recognizable landscape features, but purely for design reasons: to complement a composition of forms, either plants or other rocks. They can introduce a distinctive feature, a landmark, as a striking and powerful element of the design.

Again, rocks may be brought into the landscape to represent, at reduced scale, a famous and cherished landscape feature. In Japan, this might be Mount Fuji or islands in the Inland Sea; in America, Pikes Peak or Yosemite Rock might be represented symbolically in a garden landscape.

Above: A fitted stone retaining wall, random irregular courses, hidden mortar joints. The wall has a battered face that is superimposed by a free-standing masonry stucco wall. *Sakamoto, Shiga Prefecture*

Center: A low retaining wall of granite boulders set deeply into the ground. By overlapping each other for support and creating a more irregular configuration, the boulders create the illusion of cliffs overhanging a stream. The path's pavement consists of roof tiles set on edge with scattered flat-topped field stones. Moss grows between the joints. *Japanese garden, Westchester County, New York*

Below: Boulders overlapping each other to form a retaining wall. They suggest cliffs overlooking the banks of a river. *Zhuozhengyuan, Suzhou, China*

Another use for rocks in a garden, practiced mainly in China, is as monolithic, free-standing natural sculptures, such as the *taihu* steles frequently found in Chinese classical gardens. Or they may also have anthropomorphic or zoomorphic connotations. A most obvious example is the rock work in Shizilin (Lion Grove Garden) in Suzhou, which looks like lions cavorting in a courtyard.

Finally, we come to the fourth and most characteristic function of rocks in Japanese gardens: the use of an abstract symbol to evoke in the mind of the viewer the wide world of nature. The most notable examples are the dry *karesansui* terrains of Japan's Zen temple gardens. Daisen-in, a sub-temple within the Daitokuji temple complex, exemplifies that evocation of wilderness, of far-off mountain scenery. Here, in a confined space of roughly thirty by fifteen

Above: Quarried blocks form the retaining wall. The battered face insures that each block's center of gravity is pushing into the grade above, thereby insuring stability. *Kurodani Kōmyōji, Kyoto*

Center: Granite boulders set in irregular groupings on a hillside serve to retain the grade of the paved terrace above. Cotoneaster is the groundcover. The effect is like *sute-ishi*, scattered rocks tumbling down a hillside. *Private garden, Westchester County, New York*

Below: A retaining wall of boulders fitted together, and overlapping both horizontally and vertically. The weight of each rock, its center of gravity, is pushing back into the hillside. Although the wall suggests cantilevered, overhanging cliffs, the balance of each rock is weighing into the embankment. Joints are dry. *Nanzenji, Kyoto*

Water action has eroded the surfaces of these metamorphosed rocks. The attention drawn to the dominant rock in the grouping incisively demonstrates its importance in the composition. *Kiyosumi Teien, Tokyo*

feet, is a stunning landscape of stone and gravel, with only a few compact shrubs as background. A clear expression of Zen art it is, in effect, a striking sculptural rendering of a monochrome ink painting. This epitomization of nature in the raw has lain behind temple walls, moldering under its patina of time for over four hundred years.

Daisen-in's spare composition of craggy rocks and gravel may, in its most abstract sense, be seen as a metaphor for the cosmos. Yet it is still recognizable on its earthbound level as an expression of a remote mountain landscape. By contrast, the most remarkable example of abstraction carried to its extreme is the *karesansui* flat garden at Ryōanji. So mathematically obstruse and open to interpretation, it startles and inspires first time visitors. I, myself, shall never forget my first contact with it. Even on subsequent visits, the search for its meaning continues. What, one asks, did its creator have in mind?

But far surpassing its tendency to provoke questions is the garden's mysterious evocative powers. One gets the feeling of having encountered something rare and profoundly suggestive. In that austere space about the size of a tennis court, fifteen rocks arranged asymmetrically in a "sea" of raked gravel are able to convey a sense of limitlessness of both space and time. There is no beginning and no end. Such rock work—uniquely Japanese—becomes a mantra, inspiring spells of unanticipated meditation.

A pond garden surrounded by pavilions for the offices of a corporate headquarters. The architecture suggests the style of *shinden-zukuri* of the eleventh century (Heian Period). The pond is constructed entirely of concrete. Rocks set along the edges and groundcover plantings hide the concrete edge. The large rock grouping is a waterfall at the end of a hill peninsula jutting out into the water. *Gulf States Paper Corporation, Tuscaloosa, Alabama*

Where the swiftly flowing stream tends to eat away at the concave curves of the edge, it is guided past by blocks of cut granite which serve instead of rocks. They suggest ancient foundation stones or pilings along a waterway. The recumbent blocks suggest boat landing platforms between the upright pilings. *Nanzenji, Kyoto*

From rocks set into the hillside, a thread of water falls onto a splash rock in the shallow rock-studded pool. *Ginkakuji, Kyoto*

Above and center: Shorelines of ponds in gardens in Suzhou, China. The *taihu* rock work is integrated into the foundations of the buildings set close to the water. These were gardens for private residences, but are now open to the public. *Suzhou, China*

Below: The concentration of heavy-limbed black pines around the shores of the pond balances off the mass of rock work so that even in winter the scene does not become stark and bare. *Nijō Castle, Kyoto*

Above: A wide waterfall of shallow rapids is most effective with a high volume of flow, together with smaller rocks and gravels embedded in the stream, causing white water. It suggests a grand waterfall amid high mountains which is fed by a mighty stream. *Kōko-en, Himeji Castle, Hyōgo Prefecture*

Center and below: Suiseki miniature stone landscapes whose sharp needle-like spires suggest mountains in China. *On display in Nanjing and Chengdu, China*

Above: The large boulder set into the middle of the stream causes the water to rise at the bend, and to course more swiftly and noisily through the straits. Hence the necessity to place larger rocks upstream closer together from the choke point. The groundcovers are moss, turf grass and *sasa* (dwarf bamboo). *Kōko-en, Himeji Castle, Hyōgo Prefecture*

Center: Rocks placed in the upper stream divide the water into several ribbons which drop in a series of cascades before hitting the surface of the pond. The individual rocks scattered in front and projecting from the pond's surface give a sense of depth to viewers. *Kōko-en, Himeji Castle, Hyōgo Prefecture*

Below: In a broad waterfall the water action is quite gentle when the drop is low and the rim of the fall rock is smooth. *Kōko-en, Himeji Castle, Hyōgo Prefecture*

Above: The pine-covered island, concealing sections of the opposite shore, makes the pond seem larger. The rocks on the island, particularly those on the right, strengthen its impact yet link it to the other rock concentrations along the shore of the pond on the opposite side. One gets the sense that sometime in the past the island floated away from the mainland, breaking the connection with the other rock mass. *Kinkakuji, Kyoto*

Center: This *karesansui* garden for the *hōjō* (abbot's quarters) of the Zen temple was designed in 1938 to suggest in its four groupings legendary Elysian islands in a distant sea. As symbols in a purely abstract arrangement, their placement nicely contrasts the soaring vertical shapes of the upright rocks with the anchoring horizontal rocks conveying a sense of stability and repose. The five moss-covered hills in the far corner provide the necessary counterweight to the rocks, giving thereby an overall balance to the composition. *Tōfukuji, Kyoto*

Below: Like soft blankets, mosses and lichens gradually have enveloped the rocks, cushioning their hard edges and muffling the rocks' rough "voices." *Fuyō-en, Sakamoto, Shiga Prefecture*

THE DESIGN PROCESS

The designer-builder will never have absolute freedom in working out a design scheme with rocks. There are always constraints to the project, both budgetary and spatial. Yet, in one sense, this is a headstart. At least he is immediately guided by those considerations: a given program, a set budget, the area to be treated, functional objectives, existing features that must not, or cannot, be disturbed (buildings, trees, immovable rocks), visible features outside the project, the topography, bedrock, underground utilities, even weight limitations if the project is on a roof.

One or more of those factors are bound to exist and certainly will influence the designer in his earliest thinking. He therefore must come up with a scheme that, while working within those limitations, will at the same time create a work of art in the garden which holds the interest of the viewer, produces an emotional impact, and satisfies his longing for an evocative landscape. Of course, even without those site and budgetary considerations, the designer encounters those limiting boundaries that exist within his mind: his creative spirit, his taste, his sense of what the site deserves.

And so, having mulled over all the relevant factors, the designer now enters the most mysterious phase of the work—from nothing, from thin air, coming up with a theme, an idea, the symbolic kernel around which his design will revolve. I must admit that when I first was faced with that design process I felt a vague panic. What if I make the wrong choice? I thought. It was only after several years of experience that I approached the task, not with trepidation, but rather with confidence, even joyful anticipation, for I had accomplished the sometimes boring, but necessary, nitty-gritty consideration of all the limitations within the project. At last, I was free to start the really exciting, even thrilling, phase of first creating in my mind the ideal landscape with its rocks arranged to form the desired symbolism. I saw it all in my mind, the finished product, before a single line had been drawn on paper.

What considerations then go through the mind of the designer? On what level should the sought-after evocative symbolism be constructed? Is a more realistic representational effect desired, considering the existing site conditions, as well as the client's wishes and personality? Or would a more abstract and not immediately obvious effect be appropriate? Certainly, the simpler the design, the sparser its elements, the fewer and more ordinary the

A path along a side of the main hall of a temple. Rectangular slabs, end to end, enclose square granite pavers set point to point, and are themselves enclosed within a sea of *nachiguro* (black river pebbles). All elements are held in place in a mortar matrix on a concrete base below grade. The path is separated from the building by a drainage trough catching rain that pours from the roof eaves. The trough is filled with loose *nachiguro*, repeating the natural pebbles in the path—an elegant and expensive idea. *Ryōgen-in, Daitokuji, Kyoto*

rocks, and the greater dependence for effect on empty space, the more abstract will be the signals in the mind of the viewer. His mind will have to work harder if the rock composition is to ring bells in his head. The more the mind must "travel," the more evocative the impact. The farther the viewer sees, the more meanings will be dug out of the rock arrangements.

Once I have in mind the outline of the scheme, I then begin to draw it on paper, preparing a sketch to scale. At that stage I see for the first time my design in a plan view. It gives me my first chance to make revisions, to move features around if I deem it necessary, and to try out variations of my original concept. To get a more realistic understanding of the design, it

Above: A dry stream and waterfall in a *karesansui* garden, built over a structural concrete slab. The core of the hill is styrofoam, placed to lighten the load on the slab. The rocks are diabase found in Wisconsin. *Japanese garden, Nikko Hotel, Chicago*

Below: The intricate composition of rocks is overlorded by a tall pine tree and backed up by a wall of sheared broadleaved evergreen trees. The rocks seem to be struggling to reach a summit while the lower base rocks hold their tops horizontally to impart stability to the scene. Then the grouping increases in motion and dynamism as the higher rocks begin to lean diagonally closer to the summit. The narrow, moss-bordered path of cut stone slabs that inserts itself across the gravel "sea" injects a strong man-made order to balance the powerful impact of the rocks. *Konchi-in, Nanzenji, Kyoto*

Opposite page: A simulation of a stream, constructed of stone shards set on edge in a mortar bed, suggesting water dropping through a rocky gorge. *Private garden, Ridgefield, Connecticut*

Rocks set into the building's foundation walls connect
the man-made elements in a strong clasp with nature.
Zhuozhengyuan, Suzhou, China

often helps to make a study model. It may be built on a wood panel or stiff cardboard base, upon which I place scaled models of trees, rocks and other important elements of the design. Modeling clay is handy. Or I make a shallow tray, fill it with moist sand and use pebbles and stones selected to scale to move around and sink into the soft surface of the sandbox in whatever arrangement furthers the design. The advantage of constructing a study model is that I can quickly grasp the three-dimensional quality of the scheme. The effect is as if I were actually sitting or standing at a favorite viewing point in the garden. With most models at ¼ inch or ⅛ inch scale, in order to grasp the design's three-dimensional quality, the eyes are brought to a level a few inches above the study model.

Having made needed revisions either on paper, with a study model, or both, I then prepare a conceptual drawing for presentation to my client. It may be a colored, rendered plan showing shadows cast by the elements of the design to give the drawing a three-dimensional effect. It may be a perspective rendering. Or it may be a plan together with a model. The form the presentation takes depends upon the client's preference and capacity to grasp the concept from looking at a drawing.

The creative process has thus advanced to the execution of the design. But despite my recital of an orderly progression of phases, it should be emphasized that the creative process, as with all human efforts, never runs along a straight and swift path. There are twists and turns, halts and hesitations, reconsiderations and revisions along the way—even after site work has

Shaded by dense pines, the waterfall's source is made dark and mysterious. The large rocks evoke the feeling of high and distant mountains. *Nijō Castle, Kyoto*

A quiet, slowly moving stream flows past a low embankment covered in rounded pebbles that suggest a beach. The rocks, however, call to mind mountains along a seacoast or rocky islets in the sea. By observing the scene from behind the rocks and mounded shrubs in the foreground, the stream and the pebbly far bank appear farther away. *Nijō Castle, Kyoto*

Rocks assembled in a strong enough massing to
become one essential half of the *yin-yang* duality with
the plants. Their arrangement suggests a landscape of
distant hills and mountains. *Kurodani Kōmyōji, Kyoto*

begun. I have learned never to be afraid to change my mind if, later on, I think I have a better idea. Often, unexpected site conditions are discovered that will necessitate a change. Or, once work begins, I may see the scheme in a different light. Frequently, the rocks, once brought to the site, appear different. Perhaps they are larger or smaller than previously realized; perhaps they now suggest other possible configurations not originally foreseen. It is a poor landscape architect or garden builder who rigidly sticks to his original plan and refuses to see, as the work progresses, new and better ways of placing the rocks and other elements of the design.

I remember an experience of forty years ago while working in Japan with my mentor, Sano-sensei. We were on a garden construction project for a private residence in the mountains of Hida Takayama. It was to be a garden adjacent to a *chashitsu* (tea ceremony room). Large rocks were brought to the site, and *sensei*, with me and his workers, spent several days arranging the rocks to his satisfaction. In those days, no power lifting equipment was available. Rocks were lifted with a block and fall suspended from a tripod, and they were moved with pry bars and hand-turned windlasses and winches.

In that project, there was one particular feature rock which weighed several tons. We struggled with it for what seemed many hours before Sano-sensei said he was satisfied with its positioning, and it was dusk before we quit work for the day. He and I shared one of the large rooms in that ancient house. Exhausted after our hard day's struggle, we retired early after dinner.

It is the next morning. I wake up early and see that *sensei* has already gotten up and left the room. I quickly dress and go looking for him. At last I find the master. He is sitting on the veranda, unmoving, gazing into the garden. His eyes are focused on that multi-ton rock with which we had struggled so laboriously the day before, and which occupied such a prominent place in the design. *Sensei* looks at me: "I am still not satisfied," he says. "In the morning light I see the rock differently. We must move it forward a few feet, and turn it slightly." I am astonished. Here is the expert on garden design, a talented man with more than fifty years of experience, yet he is not sure of his earlier idea. He wants to change it.

But our client, when he sees what is happening, is thrilled. He is happy that his garden designer is putting so much thought into the creation of his garden. Concern about the increased labor cost does not enter his mind.

I realized then that here was a supreme master: an artist full of confidence in his powers of intellect and creative expression and not ashamed to change his mind. It is a lesson which, through my own forty years of work in the field, has helped me with my personal artistic convictions.

Returning to look at a rock composition of mine in a garden completed years ago, I, too, have sometimes seen the design in a different light. And I have thought I would like to make changes, but often the situation would not permit it. At least, however, my mind was open. Like Sano-sensei so many years ago, I was not afraid to admit that there could be a better way to do it.

CHAPTER SIX

ROCKS—WHERE TO FIND THEM

Once the decision is made to use natural rocks in a garden, the question arises: where to find them? In areas that were heavily glaciated, such as northern North America, one can find rocks strewn all over the landscape, either deposited as a moraine or drumlin, or simply dragged along in the ice of 10,000 years ago. Most of those glacial boulders are granites, the stone preferred for Japanese gardens.

Taihu, the most prized rock in Chinese gardens, is lifted from lakes and streams, the water action being the source of its distinctive cavities, honeycomb tunnels, crevices, and holes. It is found in the Kerrville Formation in central Texas, and karst landscapes in southern China and Yugoslavia.

Over my years of designing and building gardens with rocks, I have had to find rocks in a variety of far-flung places. For example, when our firm made a Japanese garden in Chicago for the Nikko Hotel we needed a source of rocks suitable for the garden. But since northern Illinois has few exposed rocks, it was necessary to seek them farther afield. The nearest source was in central Wisconsin. The contractor found a farm there with pastures and fields covered with rocks of different sizes and shapes scattered in easily accessible terrain.

It was, therefore, simply a matter of arranging with the contractor for a visit to meet the owner of the property.

And so, one blustery day in early winter, I flew to Wisconsin, dressed for the Arctic and armed with several lumber marking crayons (yellow or red are best in summer because they stand out against the green foliage). In fewer than three hours I had marked a sufficient quantity of rocks which, the following spring, would be trucked to Chicago.

In another instance, for a project in Tuscaloosa, Alabama, where the local stone consists mainly of shaley slabs of limestone found along stream beds, rocks for a Japanese garden were shipped from Greenwich, Connecticut in two railroad gondola cars. They came from an abandoned farm stone fence which the owner wanted to get rid of. The rocks were perfect—weathered angular granite boulders in a variety of sizes and shapes—and the wall was easily accessible. A front-end loader simply backed up to the wall where two men with crowbars pushed the rocks onto the loader bucket, which then slid them onto a waiting flatbed truck. Using slings, a crane at the railroad siding lifted the rocks from the truck and deposited them in the waiting gondola cars.

Nature's *tate-ishi. Yunnan Province, China*

Rocks situated along a stream, as found in nature. *Shiga Prefecture*

For yet another Japanese garden project in Nashville, Tennessee, where local shale limestone was not appropriate, granite boulders were sought in an abandoned utility line right-of-way, just outside of Atlanta, Georgia. After obtaining permission from the owner, I went to the site, selected and marked the rocks which were later to be shipped to Nashville.

Happily, in the northeastern United States, good rock sources are readily available and not too distant from most garden projects, particularly in areas where there was ancient glaciation. Throughout the New England states, New York, northern

New Jersey and Pennsylvania, from early colonial times onwards, farmers were faced with the necessity of clearing their fields of boulders, mostly granites, in order to do their planting. Consequently, over the course of three centuries of agricultural activity, fields were cleared regularly, mostly during winter when stone boats and sleds were drawn over the snow by teams of oxen. The rocks were then distributed in windrows along the edges of fields, where they would be readily available for farmers to build stone fences in their idle time. Since these rocks were not

Small boulders retaining a low hill in a *karesansui* garden. *Nikko Hotel, Chicago*

taken from streams, whose water action would have rounded and smoothed their surfaces, they are nicely angular. Showing many interesting facets, they are ideal for use in garden rock work that evokes the natural mountain landscapes of the world outside.

Once the garden builder becomes acquainted with the general availability and type of rock resources in his region, he must then get down to the task of locating a specific source. Where does he go to look for them? Many years ago, early in my tutelage I asked my mentor: "*Sensei*, where do you find rocks?" With crinkling eyes and a wry smile, he replied: "Rocks are where you find them." From then on, I realized the importance of keeping my eyes open while traveling through the countryside, no matter where it ultimately took me. I would make mental or written notes on rock locations wherever I found them. Driving along a road bordering woodlands, pastures, fields, an old quarry or an excavation, for instance, I would suddenly spot a potential supply of rocks.

And from time to time, at a contractor's place of business I would see rocks scattered over his back lot. He would be keeping them for future sale. Some of the rocks may have come from an excavation or blasting operation. He may have gotten them at almost no cost; the original owner would have been glad to have them taken away. All the contractor had to pay was the cost of removal from the original site. Then, years later, I show up at the contractor's place of business to select from his pile of rocks for my particular project.

Also, in the United States, many plant nurseries and garden centers are potential sources; they collect natural rocks for later sale. In Japan there are rock merchants who stock rocks in their yards. Japanese rocks, however, are often very expensive because of their long pedigrees, a history that goes back to the time when a particular rock, celebrated in paintings and poetry, occupied a prominent place in the garden of a daimyo lord, court official or famous artist. As the fortunes of that particular illustrious family waned, their property would be sold or seized. Their garden, too, may have been dismantled, and its rocks sold off to a rock dealer or expropriated by the successor lord. The more history is attached to a rock, the more expensive it becomes.

I remember once visiting the garden of a wealthy man in Kanazawa. He also dealt in rocks and stone artifacts. Showing me around his garden, he would say: "Do you see that rock? It cost me 200,000 yen. Or that rock over there, a half million. And this rock, said to come from the garden in Kyoto of General Hideyoshi, almost two million." That man was less concerned with the esthetics of his garden, than with the value of his rock collection. He felt very secure. He didn't need burglar alarms or watchdogs to protect his investment in rocks; they were too heavy to be readily stolen. And in view of the rising affluence of Japan, his rocks were growing in value day by day. For him it was as if he had invested in a stock that was continually going up in value. He was very happy.

Other Japanese may not have to seek out rocks for their gardens; a rock may be passed down the generations as part of the family inheritance and even seen as a protector of the family's fortunes. I remember once being shown around a garden on the Izu Peninsula by its owner and noticing an isolated pair of weathered granite rocks in a mossy glade. One was upright, a *tate-ishi*, about thirty inches high; the other, a prone, rounded rock. On going closer, I realized that their forms were unmistakably human genitalia, male and female, which had been shaped by nature. Smiling, I turned to my host. He gazed down on the two rocks and in a serious tone said: "These are friends of the family. They have been with us over many generations and we have prospered. My son will look after them when I am gone."

A wild setting of trees, shrubs and ferns among rocks
strewn helter-skelter, as nature left them. *Sute-ishi*
French style. *Albert Kahn Garden, Paris, France*

SELECTING ROCKS

Having found my source of rocks, I now face the most pivotal and riskiest part of the work. Many questions arise. Even before selecting individual specimens, I must ask myself what functions or esthetic goals the rocks are expected to achieve. Are they to work simply as a retaining wall, or to serve as steppingstones? Will they be placed along the banks of a rushing mountain brook or a slow, meandering stream? Or are the rocks to be set along the shoreline of a pond or a lake? And what natural landscape do I intend to evoke? A rugged mountain scene with a lofty waterfall, a series of undulating gentle hills, a sandy or gravelly beach, or a rocky island emerging from the sea? Once the intended effect becomes clear in my mind, I am ready to pick my material.

Some of the rocks are spread out over the ground, making it easy for me to spot the ones appropriate for my project. Others are buried in piles. In that case I ask the manager of the rock source to spread out the pile so that I can clearly see the rocks from all angles before making a selection. I then must think about the required sizes, shapes, colors and textures. The relationships of scale between individual rocks, the size of the area of work, and surrounding landscape features all have to

be taken into consideration. The size of the rocks also influences the delicate balance—of feeling and weight—between the growing elements of trees and shrubs and the inanimate element of rock. For instance, in the gardens of Nijō Castle, once the Kyoto residence and headquarters of the Tokugawa Shogun, the rocks are exceptionally abundant and large, imposing their dominance over the garden landscape. The impressive weight of the rocks seems to echo the power of the family for whom the garden was built three hundred years ago.

By contrast, in the gardens of Kyoto's Gosho (the palace of the Imperial family, which ruled in name only before the Meiji Restoration and the fall of the Shogunate), the rocks are fewer, smaller, and convey a gentler, quieter feeling. There, plants outweigh the rock element.

It is evident then that by manipulating scale—the size and quantity of rocks—I have the power to evoke a range of moods, and to create in the mind of the beholder a variety of natural landscapes. The character of the terrain which I aim to evoke will influence, as well, the choice of rock shapes. Representations of rugged mountain peaks and crags require sharp, angular, blocky specimens, while the gentle,

Cascades in a recirculated stream contained within a
water-tight, concrete sluiceway. The rocks set inside
the channel effectively hide the concrete, thereby conveying the impression of a natural mountain brook.
Private residence, Greenwich, Connecticut

A dressed stone retaining wall with tight joints. The stones, with their long axes laid horizontal, give the wall a sense of strength and repose. *Kurodani Kōmyōji, Kyoto*

Large natural *tobi-ishi* (steppingstones) not only become a section of a path around the edge of a pond, but also define the water's edge. They are set deeply into the earth. *Kiyosumi Teien, Tokyo*

rolling terrain of an old and distant, worn down landscape is suggested by more rounded and smoother rocks.

Perspective is also affected by color and size. If it is considered desirable to suggest greater depth and distance in the garden composition, then lighter-colored and larger rocks are placed in the foreground, close to the main viewing point. Darker-colored and smaller rocks are set farther away in the background. Rocks discolored by soil stains can be washed with pressure hoses to restore their essential color.

To create a unified rock composition, there must be a harmony of color and texture within the grouping and with adjacent rocks. Harmony would be disrupted, for instance, if white quartzite or limestone were used in compositions where the rest of the stone is dark gray weathered granite.

And so, with a definite picture in my mind of the desired effect, I set out with marking chalk crayon in hand. Like a butterfly or a bee, I move from rock to rock. Although in my mind I have a feeling for the desired effect, I do not know (nor do I care) at this stage of the selection process where each rock will precisely fit. More

Tobi-ishi are set into the concrete bed of this pebble-studded stream. The summer visitor gets the benefit of air cooled by the fast flowing water around the steppingstones yet keeps his feet dry. The large granite rocks set along the edges steer the flow around the curves and bends in the water course, and the pebble bottom creates the right amount of turbulence to make the water babble. The groundcover is moss, pine needles and *sasa* (dwarf bamboo). *Japanese garden, Westchester County, New York*

Natural and cut stone *tobi-ishi* serve as a path and define the separation between the moss and the gravelly earth in this private garden. *Ōtsu City, Shiga Prefecture*

importantly, what I do see are possibilities in each rock: its different facets, how it can be turned, which side should be the top, where is the best face, how deep it can be set, and how it may relate to rocks already selected or those yet to be encountered.

Because my mind has been programmed over years of contact with myriad rock landscapes of nature, I catch in an instant some correspondence in a particular rock with that real world: I may see the karst mountains along the Li River in Guilin, South China; the rocky coastlines of Oregon, Maine or Sri Lanka; the craggy peaks of northern Italy's Dolomites and those in the Colorado Rockies; or the rocky isles in Japan's Inland Sea. One rock can convey to me any one of a host of natural landscapes I have come upon in my travels.

Does this creative imagination naturally occur with all landscape designers? Is it something they are born with? I would say yes—with some. But even among those few, such sensibilities must be expanded and fine-tuned through experience and by exposure to nature's great landscapes. After that, learning by doing is an essential part of the training in which one must become one's sternest critic.

The large rocks set erratically along the shore provide a visual frame. The tall rocks form the points of the promontories, while smaller rocks line the coves. In effect, the large rocks at the points divide the pond into two and consequently create the illusion of a larger body of water. *Ginkakuji, Kyoto*

By extending rock placement out into the water to form a peninsula, the shoreline becomes a series of ins and outs—sheltered coves and spits—thus creating for the viewer a sense of greater space. The whole of the pond cannot be seen from any one viewpoint. *Kinkakuji, Kyoto*

Rocks set at the end of peninsulas convey the feeling of a rockbound seacoast. They strengthen the impact of the arm of land jutting out into the water, dividing the pond into sections. The water thereby appears larger than it actually is. *Nijō Castle, Kyoto*

So many large rocks along the shore make them seem closer to the viewer than they are in reality. This garden was created within the enclosed grounds of the castle residence in Kyoto for the Tokugawa Shogun. The rocks, in their large dimensions and abundance expressing pure power rather than subtlety, suggest a distant landscape of high, daunting mountains, crags and precipices—an impressive reminder of Tokugawa preeminence. *Nijō Castle, Kyoto*

Above: At close range, the viewer faces a mountain fastness with grottoes and caves in this compressed space squeezed into the hillside. The scattering of sheared azaleas and other smaller plants is balanced by the hard, strong line of the stone bridge linking the hillside to the house. Even in winter the garden attracts viewing. *Shiga-in, Sakamoto, Shiga Prefecture*

Below: A Buddha carved in bas-relief on a rock in a bamboo grove. *Japanese garden, Westchester County, New York*

Above: Stone Buddhist figures in a bamboo grove. They seem to be enjoying life in their shady setting. *Hakusasonsō, Kyoto*

Below: Granite boulders are set within a concrete gunnite shell. The water is recirculated to brim over the edge of the fall rock, which covers the upper concrete reservoir. The pine branch sweeping across the top of the falls adds mystery by obscuring the water source. *Private garden, Westchester County, New York*

Above: The granite blocks in this new garden suggest pilings along a lake or stream. At the bend in the stream, they are set in rising tiers and in depth where the water tends to eat into the higher bank. The groundcover is moss and deciduous shrubs. *Kōko-en, Himeji Castle, Hyōgo Prefecture*

Below: A sense of shallow rapids in a slow moving, meandering stream within a broad, level valley is created by the small, rounded rocks set along the edges of the stream. The low, sheared azaleas among moss and lawn evoke modest, worn down hills bordering the waterway. *Murin-an, Kyoto*

Above: Antique stone pillars in an asymmetrical grouping are placed as if they were rocks in a *karesansui* garden. The raked furrows, integral to the design, unify all the elements of the composition. *Tōfukuji, Kyoto*

Below: This recently completed garden sits within the walls of a castle, once the seat of a powerful daimyo family. The family's power is suggested by the large rocks lining the banks of the pond, reminiscent of the pond in Nijō Castle. In time, lichens, mosses and other low plants will soften the impact of the rocks. The island in the middle distance, with its rocks, represents the mythical tortoise. *Kōko-en, Himeji Castle, Hyōgo Prefecture*

Below left: Rocks of chert evoke steep cliffs. This hard, flintlike stone, especially prized and sought after by garden connoisseurs in Japan, was dug up along a stream on the owner's land. *Shiga Prefecture*

Above right: Basaltic rock from an ancient lava flow, set to keep its original horizontal inclination, as if it were still in its first fluid state. *Kiyosumi Teien, Tokyo*

Below right: A metamorphic sedimentary boulder, solidly set, suggesting a mountain. It also acts as a foil to the mass of cryptomeria trees that surround it: *yin-yang* duality in action. *Nijō Castle, Kyoto*

What comes to mind seeing this granitic rock for the
first time? A toad or head of a snake emerging from the
water? Its ridged and wrinkled surface may suggest
the skin of an animal. Whatever the image, it is a rock
with evocative powers. *Kiyosumi Teien, Tokyo*

Is it a tortoise lying on its side?
Kiyosumi Teien, Tokyo

Metamorphosed sandstone, eroded by water action, overshadows other elements in the garden, suggesting a mythic animal at rest.
Rikugi-en, Tokyo

Even alone, the rock suggests a landscape of hills and valleys. *Ryōanji, Kyoto*

The rocks' flintlike textures, scaly undulating patterns and parallel vertical seams create an archaic touch reminiscent of early Chinese and Japanese paintings. They evoke water flowing over rocks. *Private collection, Shiga Prefecture*

ROCK SETTING—STEP BY STEP

Working with rocks I feel joy, looking upon each one as a friend and ally, unresistant and compliant in taking its place wherever I want to put it. Yet this holds true only if I take the time to appreciate the rock's potentialities: I turn it over, look at it from all sides to determine its center of gravity, and assess its good and bad features. Only then can I visualize how it will fit in with the other rocks already in place or waiting for installation. On occasion, such an evaluation of a rock can take less than thirty seconds; at other times, minutes will pass before I get a clear picture of how it is to be set. Once that mental process is accomplished, however, the steps involved in installation follow a logical and orderly approach.

Assuming a rock has been selected from the storage pile or from a group dispersed over the ground, the next step is to move it closer to its final resting place and within reach of the lifting rig. If the site of the rock source and the place of its ultimate setting are close enough to be within reach of a crane or other power mechanical equipment, the rock, then and there, can be slung up in the desired attitude for its final positioning. As a saving in time and money, such an arrangement is preferable. It also incurs less wear and tear on the nerves of the director of the work since there will be shorter distances to travel and less time consumed moving back and forth between the rock assembly area and the work site. It is desirable, therefore, that the site of the rock supply be as close as possible to where the rocks are to be placed.

Although arranging rocks is creating a work of art which ideally proceeds without regard to cost, in reality, such concerns are always hovering in the back of my mind. I never use artificial rock but have to recognize that it is less expensive to move hollow fiberglass boulders or to cast in place concrete in rubber molds than to engage mechanical lifting rigs to place heavy natural rocks. Time spent and charges for mechanical equipment add to the expenses. Acting not only as artist-creator-technician-director but also as protector of the client's budget, I must insure that the work is performed as economically as possible without jeopardizing the finished product.

The order of the placement of the rocks cannot be determined in advance. It must be one rock at a time. As each rock is positioned, I step back to gaze upon the work. I gauge the rock's height, attitude, surfaces, convexities and concavities. Only

A boulder being moved while hitched to a chain sling. Suspended from the bucket of a front-end loader, it is being carried to its ultimate placement. Note the slip hook at the choke hitch, keeping the rock snugly held by the sling until it is lowered into position. *Private garden, Moosehead Lake, Maine*

Granite boulders waiting to be placed. Note their scale compared to the size of a man. *Private garden, Putnam County, New York*

then, all the while keeping in mind an image of the rock just previously installed, can I hurry back over to the rock assembly area, survey the field of choice realistically, and decide on the next rock to be picked up and put into place. If the source is close by, a crane can swing around to pick it up. A somewhat less flexible mechanical mover is the telescopic arm of an excavator, a backhoe or a front end loader with a hook on the bucket. If there is no hook, slings can also be suspended on the teeth of the bucket.

Before slinging up the rock, I must decide which should be the top and face of the rock—which side is up and which side is to have the optimum exposure. It is a reciprocal, with each decision affecting another. In choosing the face, I select the facet whose form, surface texture, lines, striations, indentations and ridges most clearly and vividly evoke, in reduced scale, the sought-after effect: perhaps a rugged mountain peak, a section of mountain range, or a gentle rolling hill. And with a flat-topped rock, to convey a sense of stability and repose, I want its horizontal plane to be set as level as possible. It is as if each rock matches or brings to mind a swatch, a fragmentary piece of an actual ridge, peak or hill seen in my past travels which has become imprinted upon my memory. An unconscious click occurs in my brain. I know, beyond any doubt, that that particular rock fits in and takes its place as part of the completed landscape my imagination sees in the rocks on the ground before me.

Having selected a rock for placement, established its top and face, and determined its position in the composition, I must next decide on the best method of setting the rock in place. I have achieved the greatest control in precise placement by putting the rock in a steel chain sling to lift it into place. In determining the fitting and adjustment of the sling around the rock, I make an initial judgment on the location of the rock's center of gravity. Judging this aids in the precise fitting of the sling around the rock. And, as natural rocks and boulders are generally irregularly shaped, often narrow on one side and broader on the opposite end, the rock naturally will be heavier where it is wider or fatter. To compensate for that difference, and to maintain the top of the rock level as it is set (if that is the desired effect), the hitch of the sling must be moved closer to the heavy end, where the rock's center of gravity will be found. Thus, when lifted, the rock will be evenly balanced, and its top surface approximately level.

The rock of flinty chert suggests rapids and falls of water flowing down a broad stream and is especially evocative when wet. *Private collection, Shiga Prefecture*

At this point the novice in rock work may very well be mystified by the concept of "center of gravity" in a rock. What does it mean? What is its importance? How do you find it? When I first started working with rocks, I, too, felt at a loss to understand its significance. Simply put, it is that spot in the interior of any mass or object where the object's point of equilibrium is found, where the weight of its mass is perfectly balanced. In a symmetrical object, such as a cube, there is no difficulty; the center of gravity has to be in its exact center. But in an irregular object—a rock, for example—you wonder how to find its center. My teacher, Sano-sensei, explained it by handing me a ten foot length of bamboo. "Hold it so that is balanced on your hand," he instructed. Seeing that a culm of

Rocks set in an irregular "in-and-out" pattern on a deep gravel base to retain a steep embankment along the shoreline of a pond. Ultimately, the water level will be raised two feet higher to cover the boulders' "feet." *Private residence, Ellicottville, New York*

A waterfall under construction. The large boulders are set directly into the earth. The water level will reach above the rocks' bottoms. The single rock set out into the water breaks up the space between the waterfall and viewers on the opposite shore. *Private garden, Putnam County, New York*

bamboo is slightly thicker at the end growing closer to the ground, I knew that the end with the wider caliper would be heavier. Allowing for that additional weight, I therefore held the pole not at the middle, but at the point where it felt balanced in my hand (4½ feet from the heavier end and 5½ feet from the narrower end). *Sensei* was pleased. "It is the same principle in judging a rock's center of gravity," he said. "The hitch of the sling is placed at that point on the rock where you will find the rock's balance."

As my experience with rock work increased, I became more adept at quickly judging the center of gravity. Now I am usually within a fraction of an inch in indicating where the hitch of the sling should be placed. Knowing the rock's center of gravity allows me to get it slung up and held in the attitude I want—though not always. It is a kind of developed intuition that becomes refined with experience.

Even when the desired effect is to emphasize a point or peak of a rock pointing skyward, the rock still must be inclined so that the peak is also in an angle of repose. The peak of the rock should look stable, equally balanced, unless the rock is purposely tilted to impart a delicate or dynamic feeling. It should not look as if it may topple over. Never in nature does a mountain appear to be trembling in the balance. It looks solid, unmoving, eternally in place. When constructing a line of rocks or boulders as a retaining wall or revetment, the tops of most of the rocks should show a level, horizontal plane to give the wall or grouping a sense of stability and repose.

Once the rock's center of gravity has been judged, the sling is fitted around the rock so that when tightened, the rock is snugly held at the desired height, attitude and lateral position as it is lowered into place. It must be placed so that the rock cannot slip out of the sling before it reaches its final position in the ground. A variety of materials is used as slings: steel chains, steel cables, ropes, nylon webbing. But for me, steel chain slings have worked out best. They are the most flexible, safest and easiest to use and provide the most control in positioning the rock. While steel cables are also safe, they are not as flexible. Their strands, moreover, tend to fray over time, often piercing the hands and fingers of the worker on the ground. Where scarring of the rocks must be avoided, slings of nylon webbing are used.

No matter what material the sling is made from, one end of the sling must have a sliding hook (choke hook) or loop attached. When the rock is raised from the ground this tightens down on the sling at the hitch as tension is exerted on the sling by the hoisting mechanism. With safety precautions in mind, before any sling is used it should be examined for its soundness. It is absolutely necessary to reject frayed cables and webbing, and chains which have weak links, are extremely rusted or of too thin a gauge and consequently too weak to cope with the weight of the rock.

To place the sling, one end of the rock is raised so that the sling can be fitted around it. If a backhoe or excavator is the lifting mechanism, the rock may be raised by the bucket on the lifter arm gently nudging its teeth under one end of the rock and raising it slightly, thereby enabling the worker on the ground to slip the sling under the rock. With the bucket still holding one end off the ground, the worker fixes the sling securely around the rock while making sure that the choke hook is placed at that point on the rock most conducive to maneuvering it into the desired inclination. For this step, if no backhoe or other power lifting rig is used, the worker may have to raise one end of the rock using a pry bar or length of timber as a lever and a rock or wood block as a fulcrum. When adjusting the sling, I always take the time to make sure that the rock is suspended in the proper attitude before placing it, rather than try to do the adjustment after the rock is lowered into place.

Once the rock is lifted into the air, it is conveyed to the earth pocket which has already been prepared to receive it. By this time I have decided how much of the rock I want exposed above the finished grade. I have measured how much of the rock will be buried, and have had the earth pocket dug to my precise measurements. For ease of maneuvering it is always advisable to make the hole bigger than the rock, for it is much easier to backfill around the rock than to have to lift it out of the hole for enlargement by additional excavation. Here again, it is a matter of economy of time.

When the rock is suspended by the sling in its final attitude, the configuration of the rock's bottom can be accurately gauged. If the rock's bottom is level, the bottom of the hole must also be level so that it can be snugly seated. On the other hand, if the bottom of the rock is lopsided and the surface slanted, then the hole must be dug to conform to this, with one end of the hole deeper than the other.

As the rock is gently lowered into the hole, I watch closely to see that it is assuming the appropriate attitude and location to achieve the intended design effect. If it is too low, the rock must be raised, and more backfill placed in the hole. Or, if it is too high, it must be lifted to allow more soil to be dug out. If the rock is not turned or inclined to my satisfaction, it must be lifted out and repositioned to the left or right, backward or forward until I see it as I first envisioned in the composition. As long as the sling remains tightly hugging the rock, such adjustments may be readily accomplished. They are made by easing the rock back into the hole; lowering the lifting arm to release the tension in the sling; moving the choking hook at the hitch to the left or right, to the rear or forward; and then once again tensioning the sling by raising the rock and lowering it into its repositioned attitude. Such adjustments, using the power of the lifting arm, in the long run save time and reduce the physical exertion and frustration of the workers on the ground.

With the rock in its final position, the next step is to withdraw the sling from underneath the rock. This is a delicate process; if not done properly, it can upset or move the rock and consequently require that it be re-slung, removed from the hole, and once again put through the placement operation to reposition it. This hazard can be minimized even before the rock is placed in position by removing from its bottom, if possible, any sharp protrusions that might snag the sling as it is withdrawn. If the ground is hard, a deeper groove should be dug in the bottom of the hole at the point where the sling will come into contact with the earth. Also, it can be helpful to raise one end of the rock, especially if the bottom is lopsided, by placing a rock or a lump of compacted soil as a block underneath the higher part. Thus, when the rock comes to rest in the hole, there remains a gap between the sling and the earth, allowing the sling to be easily withdrawn without upsetting the rock. When the ground is soft beneath the rock, a block or depressed groove is often not necessary as an aid to removal of the sling.

Another precaution to avoid upsetting the rock is to withdraw the end of the sling with the smaller hook (the hook connecting it to the lifting mechanism, not the larger choking hook) from underneath the rock. In that way there is less of a possibility it will be snagged. Tugging should first be tried simply using manpower. The tension should be held as close as possible to ground level. If the bucket of the lifting

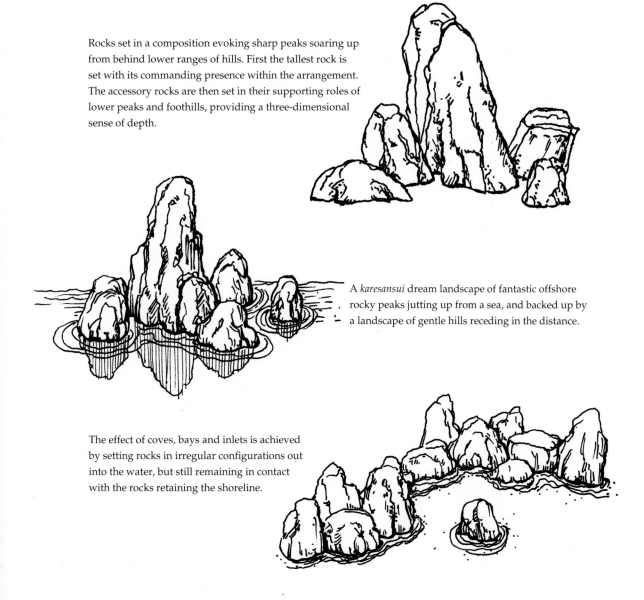

Rocks set in a composition evoking sharp peaks soaring up from behind lower ranges of hills. First the tallest rock is set with its commanding presence within the arrangement. The accessory rocks are then set in their supporting roles of lower peaks and foothills, providing a three-dimensional sense of depth.

A *karesansui* dream landscape of fantastic offshore rocky peaks jutting up from a sea, and backed up by a landscape of gentle hills receding in the distance.

The effect of coves, bays and inlets is achieved by setting rocks in irregular configurations out into the water, but still remaining in contact with the rocks retaining the shoreline.

These dominant *tate-ishi* (upright rocks), with their sheer, assertive postures, would appear lame and pointless if not supported and stabilized by recumbent rocks in their subordinate but complementary roles. As if they were animate creatures, the rocks live together in symbiotic communities. An inherent reciprocity dwells within each grouping.

Each rock takes its place as an essential element of the artist-designer's composition on the ground. An artist goes through an analogous process when-composing a picture. There is, of course, one critical difference: the rock artist works in three dimensions, operating within a wider scope—physical as well as optical. He accepts the challenge not only of creating an expressive work of art, but also of altering the viewer's perception of space and time. For example, he places tall, imposing rocks in the foreground so

that the background seems to recede. He knows also that placing *tate-ishi* in the middle distance divides the space, thereby making it appear larger.

Beyond simply appreciating the deftly composed abstract character of a rock grouping, the viewer may discover a more subjective dimension. His mind begins to travel to other realms. He may see in them a vast desert landscape of stark monoliths and low tablelands, a Stonehenge type of ancient ceremonial altars, islands in tranquil waters. He may even see human figures: several generations on a family outing, or a teacher addressing his rapt disciples.

Where the viewer "travels" or what he "sees" is of lesser importance. Rather, the unique value is in the composition's power to stimulate the imagination, to evoke a mind-expanding response. In that sense, space and time become distorted for the viewer.

The shores of a drained pond in a Japanese garden, revealing the bases of the rocks on concrete pedestals. Since the water in the pond is recirculated from a brook in a closed system, the pond is watertight as if it were a concrete pool. *Japanese garden, Westchester County, New York*

rig is used to exert more pulling tension, it too should be kept as low and horizontal as possible. Even if the sling is not snagged, one must never pull upward. Vertical, instead of horizontal, tension can upset or move the rock. As a final precaution before extracting the sling, sufficient backfill should be placed around the rock so that it is supported in place during this crucial operation.

These procedures are applicable when setting rocks in soil. However, if rocks are to be set upon a hard base, such as a concrete slab, then I must, from the very beginning, select rocks in sizes which approximate my concept of the composition of the arrangement. There will not be the advantage of working on a soft earth base that permits seating rocks into the ground at whatever heights are required by the design. And when setting rocks around the inside of a pool, I must first take into account the ultimate water level to determine how much of each rock should project above the water line. When working above the hard base of a concrete slab or pool, rocks may be lifted with slings and power equipment wherever such devices have access to the site. In addition, there should also be on hand a mason with cement and trowel at the ready.

Once the rock is positioned at the desired height and inclination, concrete blocks, supporting rocks, stone shims and wedges are placed underneath and cemented in place. Sufficient clearance space is left under the rock so that the sling may be unhitched and withdrawn without upsetting the rock. A day or so after the first cementing is done to hold the supporting rocks and wedges together, a final plastering of cement is applied below the water line around the base of the rocks, so that there appears to be a smooth and natural transition following the contours of the rock from its bottom down to the floor of the pool. In that way, when the pool is filled with water, the rock appears to extend to the pool bottom as one solid mass of stone.

Where the setting site of large rocks is inaccessible to power lifting equipment, a tripod and a block and fall, as well as hand-powered winches and windlasses may be used to lift the rocks into place. Smaller rocks—rocks of up to three hundred pounds—may be moved to the setting site in a balloon-tire nursery tree ball mover, then man-handled into place, using a pry bar or timber as a lever and wood blocks as fulcrums.

In all operations where massive rocks weighing tons are being moved, lifted and manipulated, there are hazards to be aware of, and precautions and safety measures to be followed. Above all, I always make sure that workers stand clear of a rock while it is in the air, before coming to rest in its earth pocket or on a hard base. When guiding it by hand, the worker on the ground should always be in a position of readiness, so that if the sling breaks, the rock slips from the sling, or for any other reason it drops, he may quickly get out of the way. Hands and feet must be able to be immediately withdrawn. As I mentioned earlier, at the start of operations I examine all slings for defects, and I reject those that are even remotely questionable. This rule cannot be overemphasized.

Once set in firm ground or on a hard base, the rock should not budge, regard-

A rockery and garden pool under construction. The rocks are set all around inside the concrete shell so that when completed and filled with water, the man-made shell will not be visible. It will appear as a natural pond in a rocky basin. *Nanjing, China*

A simplified redrawing of a *karesansui* temple garden from a sketch in the Edo Period garden book *To rinsen meisho zue*. I asked myself: Why did the author show this garden? What design principles does it illustrate? I find several points of interest:

(1) When only a few rocks are used to form a composition, one must be particularly discriminating in selecting them for their evocative power. Here, the two main rocks alone, with all their multi-tiered ledges, suggest entire mountain ranges.

(2) Such special rocks must not have a competing and distracting background or peripheral elements. Thus, the plants are sheared into simple hemispheric shapes to suggest gentle, receding hills, a fitting contrast to the rocks' jagged, angular profiles. The rocks are set off also by the plain background of the low white stucco wall.

(3) The scene is enhanced by the distant views of woods, field and hills—*shakkei* (borrowed landscape)—which become part of the garden composition. The two picturesque pines framing the interior garden link the foreground to the pines beyond the wall.

A significant design point in this domestic garden is
the use of the rocks to manipulate perspective—how
the space is perceived from the *tatami* room and
engawa, the principal viewpoints. The two massive
standing rocks nearest to the house make the background elements—rocks, trees and shrubs—appear to
be much farther away. Large objects look closer. The
whole scene acquires more depth. *To rinsen meisho zue*
(Pictorial encyclopedia of notable gardens in the capital)

This series of waterfalls was constructed within a grottolike cavity carved out of a hillside. Its almost vertical walls are retained by immense boulders, some weighing up to 25 tons, which were lifted into place by cranes. Water drops twelve feet from the rim of the upper fall rock into a rock-lined concrete pool, then flows over lower fall rocks into a stream below. Access to the grotto is down stone steps and over steppingstones across the pool. Even on the hottest day, it is cool within the grotto's shady, humid atmosphere. Moss and lichens cover the rocks, and the sound of the water is thunderous. *Japanese garden, Westchester County, New York*

less of pressure from frost, water action, earth movement or gravitational pull. With free-standing rocks, this can be assured by setting them at an evenly balanced angle of repose, and in an earth pocket that securely holds each one in place. When setting boulders and rocks to serve as earth-retaining walls, the center of gravity of each rock should be inclined or canted upwards by tilting it back. The stability of the boulder wall is further reinforced by each rock keeping in contact with and partially masking the rock adjacent, thereby providing support to each other. Such rocks should never be set simply lined up side by side, butting against each other. Instead, the wall's alignment will look more natural if it follows a convex and concave course.

Rock setting has become for me an intellectual and even a spiritual process. I think of it, not as a struggle in which I am pitting my wits and strengths against the rock, but rather as a cooperative partnership in which I am helping the rock to find its most evocative posture. It is satisfying, even fun, provided the actors on the ground follow Archimedes' tried and true rules of leverage, as well as those principles propounded by the Japanese masters of judo. Both used gravity as a friend, allowing the weight or momentum of a moving object to seek its own repose. "Give me a pole long enough, and a place to stand," said Archimedes, "and I will move the world."

Detail of boulders overlapped to form a stable and naturalistic retaining wall. *Private garden, Ridgefield, Connecticut*

THE FINISHING TOUCH
PATHS, PAVEMENTS, ARTIFACTS

From earliest time, man has appreciated rock not only in its natural forms, but he has also seen in that hard, relatively impervious material the possibility of working it into his own designs to create lasting objects. And so stone has been quarried, split, cut, sawn, sliced, carved, hammered, polished.

In gardens, aside from stone's use as natural boulders, it is also used to make pavements, paths with steppingstones, paver slabs, and edgings in both natural and man-made geometries. Consider also stone artifacts in a garden: bridges, towers, water basins, wellheads, sculpture.

There can be no dispute that we prefer stone for all the man-made objects in our landscape. In its solidity, it conveys a sense of steadfastness and authenticity.

In Japanese gardens, paths and pavement treatments use a wide range of stone shapes and sizes: rectangular cut stones, natural stones (sometimes termed "field stones") with at least one flat face, combinations of cut and natural stones, antique millstones, and stone pediments that were once footings for wood columns in old buildings.

Generally, the formal entrance paths and pavements of temples, shrines and important buildings are constructed of durable granite cut stone slabs which are set embedded in stable beds and have closely fitted joints. The path widths have generous proportions and can accommodate large groups of people walking several abreast. The cut stone slabs have a rough surface (bush-hammered and pitted) to prevent people slipping when wet. The paths are set two to three inches above the surrounding grade. They are also slightly pitched or crowned to facilitate quick water drainage and to prevent soil deposits encroaching onto the pavement.

Once the visitor passes over the front entranceway into the deeper precincts of the land and the garden within the property, pavement formality gives way to narrower and more informal paths, such as *tobi-ishi* (steppingstones) and *nobedan* (stone carpet) of myriad configurations and sizes. These informal pavers, with their irregularity and narrower joint spacing, usually cause the visitor to slow his pace. And that is the very reaction the garden designer intends. A visitor is expected to pause often to view the garden from different angles as he proceeds along a path.

Stone artifacts—lanterns, water basins, bridges, wellheads, towers and sculptures—introduce an expression of the human mind and spirit into a garden. But

A *tachigata*-type stone lantern (*ishi-dōrō*). Ryōanji, Kyoto

Above: This is the most casual of paths; the edges are completely irregular as if they have been eroded. The mixture of large and small steppingstones, though nicely fitted together, presents an overall impression of nonchalance and informality. *Kyoto*

Below: The steppingstone path consists of a variety of pavers: natural stones, cut stones, and round stone discs which once served as pediments supporting wood columns in ancient buildings. *Private residence, Akō, Hyōgo Prefecture*

they must be used with restraint and placed with care, so as not to overwhelm the essential naturalism of the landscape. They should not introduce a distracting or discordant note into the landscape. Choose artifacts devoid of excessive ornamentation and with simple lines, shapes, and muted tones that blend well with the rocks. As time passes, the effect of weathering upon their rough surfaces produces a tonal harmony which is accentuated by the accretions of lichen and moss. Such gradual changes are manifestations of *sabi* and *wabi*, qualities appreciated by Japanese sensibilities.

Rather than be merely decorative frills, artifacts should be honest works of craftsmanship and able to stand alone, whether they serve a functional purpose (such as a lantern, a basin or a bridge), or are simply evocative sculptures. Above all, each piece must act as an integral element of the garden's overall design, so that if it were removed, the landscape would suffer; it would lose a needed symbol of the artistry of man in partnership with nature.

Above: Closely grouped *tobi-ishi* effectively become a raised stone carpet "runner" in the garden of a private residence. *Akō, Hyōgo Prefecture*

Below: A path running along one side of an enclosed *karesansui* garden. The squared granite pavers alternate orientation between horizontal and diagonal. Rounded river pebbles surrounding the pavers are edged by granite slabs. Both pavers and edgers are set on concrete slush beds to prevent movement. *Japanese garden, Westchester County, New York*

An irregular paved path in a private garden, now
open to the public. A combination of large steppingstones with pebbles, as in the path in Kiyosumi Teien,
but narrower and with widely spaced *tobi-ishi* randomly oriented. *Hakusasonsō, Kyoto*

A path of square-cut granite pavers set in triple file and bordered by slabs set end to end. There are no cross joints. With this design it is possible to have a noticeably high crown running down the center of the path, thus facilitating quick water run-off. *Daitokuji, Kyoto*

The wide joints separating the interior pavers in myriad sizes, shapes and orientations seem to be poking fun at the sober, regimented lines of the slab borders. Is it a Zen hint that one must view the garden lying ahead with a less-than-serious mind set? *Konchi-in, Nanzenji, Kyoto*

A path of flat-faced, irregular stones bordered by straight granite slabs which sharply define the path's straight course. With no snow in the wide joints, the full effect of the pattern is revealed. The mood is transitional, midway between formal and informal. *Daitokuji, Kyoto*

The stone pavers progress into slightly more informal shapes and a wider range of sizes. The border stones have irregular interior edges, while the outside edges maintain a uniformly straight line. The stones have closely fitted joints despite the random rectangular pattern.
Kōtō-in, Daitokuji, Kyoto

The simplest formal design for a paved stone path: rectangular granite slabs set transversely, and bordered by granite slabs set end to end.
Daitokuji, Kyoto

The square granite pavers, set point to point, are surrounded by tamped earth enclosed within granite slab borders. *Tenju-an, Nanzenji, Kyoto*

Above: In a path where the material changes from regular geometric units, such as the granite cobblestones here, to natural fieldstones used as *tobi-ishi*, it is important not to make the transition abruptly from one material to the other. Rather, each material should be gradually and imperceptibly introduced into the other. Thus, a strong, natural bond is created. *Japanese garden, Westchester County, New York*

Center: Though bordered by cut granite slabs, the interior pavers are random irregular natural stones set with wider, deeper joints. The unmelted snow in the joints accentuates the irregularity of the natural stone pavers. *Ryōgen-in, Daitokuji, Kyoto*

Below: Here the stone path is also bordered by stone slabs set end to end. But the interior pavers are cut in blunt wedge shapes reminiscent of a path at Katsura Rikyū. There are no cross joints. *Daitokuji, Kyoto*

Above: A bridge of two fitted stone slabs spanning the neck of a pond and supported by natural rocks. *Rikugi-en, Tokyo*

Below: A bridge of one curved granite slab over a garden stream. The sheared azaleas along the sides suggest hills receding into the distance. *Japanese garden, Westchester County, New York*

Above and below: Natural fieldstones form a depressed enclosure—the "sea"—in which is set a stone water basin fed by a bamboo trough. Black, river-washed *nachiguro* pebbles cover the surface of the "sea." Stone slabs in the foreground provide a place to stand while dipping one's hands into the water. The *ishi-dōrō* stone lantern lights the way after dark. *Japanese garden, Westchester County, New York*

Above: A single stone slab bridge across the narrow neck of a garden pond. *Hakusasonsō, Kyoto*

Below: The encrustation of lichens and shrouds of moss on the rocks impart an air of *sabi*, the graceful patina of age. *Fuyō-en, Sakamoto, Shiga Prefecture*

Above: A *tsukubai* water basin and stone lantern where garden visitors may freshen their hands. *Kiyosumi Teien, Tokyo*

Below: A *tsukubai* water basin piped from the bottom so that water brims over the top and wets the sides. Some sides are polished; some, left rough and natural, inviting visitors to touch. Sculpture by Isamu Noguchi. *Noguchi Museum Garden, New York City*

Above: An *okigata*-type stone lantern (*ishi-dōrō*). *Fuyō-en, Sakamoto, Shiga Prefecture*

Below: Buddhist figures carved in bas-relief on the granite steles overlooking a temple graveyard. *Saikyōji, Sakamoto, Shiga Prefecture*

Above: A *chōzubachi* water basin is fed by a bamboo spout. The steppingstone in front is set close to the basin to enable a visitor to approach near enough to wet his hands. *Ryōanji, Kyoto*

Below: An *ido* stone wellhead. *Japanese garden, Westchester County, New York*

Above: A *suiseki* miniature stone landscape set inside a granite basin, placed by the entrance of a gallery of Asian art. *Ridgefield, Connecticut*

Below: An interior garden arrangement of rocks and granite *tsukubai,* piped so that water brims over the top, falling into the pebbly "sea." *Nikko Hotel, Chicago*

Above and below: Sculpture by Isamu Noguchi.
Noguchi Museum Garden, New York City

AFTERWORD

There must be no hesitancy in pointing out the value of rocks when asked "Why go to all that expense?" Is it enough to reply "They introduce a deeper and wider dimension into your life, on both conscious and unconscious levels"? Yes. Absolutely.

Rocks impart a sense of substance and wholeness into your landscape; they are solid reminders of your resolve to cope with an unpredictable universe. Every time you gaze into your garden, you will be confronted with those firm elements of reality, that combination of plants and rocks previously missing which makes up the *yin-yang* duality. The rocks loom large as the stuff of creation, the hard matter formed when the gasses cooled eons after the "big bang." They are the palpable embodiment of time past, the token reminder of when it all started.

I stand among the rocks in my garden. They breathe with the seasons and weather with time. Age darkens them. Lichens and moss make their home upon them. They are the mute but faithful witnesses to the passage of the hours, days, seasons and years. They cast an anchor out into the ceaselessly flowing stream of time.

DESIGN TIPS—GETTING STARTED

Before embarking upon creating your own garden, you can develop your awareness of rocks and their use in a number of ways.

Observing nature not only improves your eye for rocks, but also, as discussed in Chapter Two, creates that all-important mental reservoir of images. The more landscapes that are imprinted upon your memory, the more potential you will be able to see in a rock, and the more versatile you will be in composing a design.

Visits to exemplary garden rock work are another source of inspiration. It is never too late to learn from the work of others.

Reading books on Taoism and Zen helps to elucidate the philosophical rationale behind Oriental rock work. A study of the principles laid down in early Japanese and Chinese garden-making manuals is also well worth the investment of time.

I would advise the beginner, however, not to become so daunted by injunctions and prescriptions propounded nine hundred years ago that he slavishly follows rules which may not always apply. I understand the reasoning and spirit underlying the principles set forth in the twelfth-century *Sakuteiki* (The book of Japanese garden secrets), for example. But I apply these principles only when they are relevant to a particular project and its site. The acid test is to ask yourself the question: does the rock composition evoke the desired response?

The best way to learn, of course, is by doing. I would therefore recommend any potentially serious garden artist to serve an apprenticeship with a master garden designer-builder. If this is impossible in your own country, you could always find an exemplary teacher in Japan, as I did many years ago.

The following are tips for when you start work upon your garden. They are for reference only, not to be strictly adhered to. Just remember: do not lose your first inspiration—it may just be your best.

Positioning Rocks

1. Do not place sideways a rock which in nature stood upright, or vice versa. This taboo exists merely to make sure that rocks fit their ultimate purpose. Thus, if you want to create the effect of deep mountains, you would use pointed, craggy rocks. The effect of waterworn rocks along a stream or body of water would be achieved using rocks with smooth, rounded shapes and surfaces.

2. Avoid placing a long stone in a vertical

position if when stood up, it shows horizontal running seams.

3. If a principal rock has the desired upper end summit but a lower section that is not acceptable, it may still be used because its bottom part can be hidden by other rocks placed around it.

4. Tall rocks are usually used only at waterfalls, the ends of islands, and as mountains.[†]

5. The soil around an upright rock must be well tamped to insure that it is firmly anchored into the ground. But if no rocks are placed in front, it will look weak.

6. If a rock is set under a tree or against a shrub, remember not to allow the plants to grow to the point that they spoil the view of the rock.

7. Do not set rocks so that they appear too abrupt, assertive or contrived. Better to place them in a manner that seems vague and understated. In other words, the designer-builder's ego should not be too evident.[†]

8. If cost factors necessitate the use of artificial rocks, they should be placed in the background and far from the viewer. Nevertheless, one natural rock properly placed may still be better than three artificial ones.

Rock Groupings

9. A rock composition should be harmonious in color, texture and form. This makes the grouping unified as a whole.

10. One rock should dominate within a grouping.

The columns supporting the overhanging *engawa* veranda are set into cups carved into the tops of the boulders. *Japanese garden, Westchester County, New York*

A sedimentary rock set so that its seams remain horizontal, precisely as deposited eons earlier. *Rikugi-en, Tokyo*

Tobi-ishi cemented into the pebble-studded bed of a stream. *Japanese garden, Westchester County, New York*

The level tops of the rocks impart a feeling of stability and repose, strengthened by the moldering mosses and lichens which provide the sought-after qualities of *sabi* and *wabi*. *Fuyō-en, Sakamoto, Shiga Prefecture*

11. The largest rock is generally placed first. You will then be able to place the remaining lesser rocks as the composition develops. It may, however, be necessary to set a supporting rock first if its intended setting would not be easily accessible to the lifting mechanism later.

12. In a rock grouping seen from several viewpoints, avoid concentrating only on the front view. Rather, it should be a three-dimensional composition with evocative views from the sides as well as the front.

13. When a rock stands alone, place other rocks to follow it.[†]

14. If a rock is set to lean, place other rocks in the opposite direction to visually support it.[†]

15. Distance from the viewer is enhanced when far rocks are standing and near rocks are recumbent.

16. On a hillside, rocks may be set to look as if they tumbled down the hill.[†]

Setting Rocks In & Around Water

17. When setting rocks at the water's edge, keep in mind the ultimate water level. The rocks should not look like they have been submerged in a flood but, on the other hand, their "feet" (base) should not be exposed above the normal water level.

18. There should be a pitch of at least 3-4% to cause a stream to flow in a garden.

19. Do not place a rock in the exact center of a stream, but to one side, so as not to split the current equally.[†]

20. If you place a rock in a stream bed, place another rock nearby on an opposite bank.[†]

21. Side rocks set into the banks of a stream (*mizugoshi-ishi*) cause turbulence in the water.†

22. If you want to make the bend in a rushing stream look natural, set rocks jutting into the current where it would appear that the current could not demolish the rock and was therefore forced to turn, causing turbulence.

23. Do not use many rocks along a stream that meanders through a generally flat, level terrain.

24. On almost-level, flat terrain, a slow-moving, shallow stream creates interest through the colors of rocks and plantings and the subtle sounds of flowing water.

25. To make a stream appear to be in a broad valley, its source should appear to have emerged from a narrow split between two rocks.†

26. If you want a garden to suggest braided streams flowing through a broad valley, place many small rocks along their banks, especially flat, smooth rocks. They will make the water flow smoothly.

27. Ponds should not be dug too deep. Doing so is believed to cause fish to grow big and turn into harmful demons! †

28. Rocks on islands in a pond (either in water or in a *karesansui* composition) should be set at different heights.

29. When a large rock is set in a pond, the supporting stones around its base should be under water and not visible.†

30. When the sea is suggested in a pond, it must be viewed through narrow openings between hills or mountains. Do not show a vast ocean without framing the view.

The shoreline is gently defined by plantings, small rocks and wood pilings, with only a few larger rocks set along its edges. This garden, built for the residence of a painter of intense artistic sensibility, is an expression of quiet and calmness. *Hakusasonsō, Kyoto*

A path of large flat *tobi-ishi*, surrounded by small natural stones with exposed flat surfaces set into tamped earth. The steppingstones are placed transversely to the axis of the path in a zigzag formation. This is a high traffic path in a public garden, hence the unusually large sizes of the *tobi-ishi*, two to three feet long. *Kiyosumi Teien, Tokyo*

This *karesansui* garden in a quiet, unassertive style contains the essential and inseparable elements of *yin* and *yang*: small rocks and plants typically disposed in a triangular arrangement. The rock base of the white plaster side wall reinforces the impact of the rocks within the rectangle of gravel. *Ginkakuji, Kyoto*

Waterfalls in gardens can evoke visions of water falling from distant, misty peaks. Here, the ribbon of water splashes onto a rock that suggests a fish struggling to swim upstream—a symbol of fortitude and courage. *Kinkakuji, Kyoto*

31. For a seashore landscape, rocks should be rugged and disposed in an irregular, disordered pattern—a stormy arrangement evoking the turbulence of waves and high seas.

32. In building a waterfall with a drop of three to four feet, use rocks that are rugged to give it a feeling of mountains. Start building from the bottom up. The fall will look more interesting if the water tumbles down in a series of drops—each placed laterally off-center so that the water follows a zig-zag course. Side rocks are important because they guide the water and can create the desired agitation and boiling effect.

33. A waterfall should appear suddenly as if from a dark, hidden place, like a natural spring.†

34. Even in high falls of more than ten feet, construction must start from the bottom up. Before setting any rocks, a thick blanket of argillaceous clay or other water-holding membrane should be spread over the whole area of the rock work.

35. At the bottom of a waterfall after the water has passed over low splash rocks, the flow instantly becomes calm. Therefore, the rocks around the edge should be smoother and flatter, suggesting a quiet pool.

36. For a fall of many ribbons of water, the rim should be wide enough to accommodate the placement of rocks in the stream bed to divide the current and to cause the water to bounce off the rocks as it gushes past them and falls over the rim.†

37. Where a stream gradient is steep, water can be made to appear turbulent

showing white water by placing gravels and small sharp rocks where it flows rapidly. In "rock and sand" gardens, turbulence and ripples are suggested by furrows in the "sand."

38. A garden waterfall (three to four feet high) appears more natural if the width of the fall rock (the lip of the drop) is no wider than two feet. If the fall is made too wide it looks like a dam.

39. If a veranda extends over water, the supporting posts should be set into cut-out recesses on top of large natural boulders projecting above the water level.

40. Place rocks around the base of a bridge to hide its abutments.

Paths & Steppingstones

41. Set *tobi-ishi* so that the long axis of each stone is perpendicular (transversely) to the axis of the path. A path of long steppingstones, plus or minus two feet, should be set with their centers on the center line of the path. Smaller steppingstones, however, should be set zig-zag on the center line.

42. If you want visitors to slow down while walking over steppingstones, set them with narrow joints (four to five inches apart). Conversely, wide joints (six to twelve inches apart) induce a faster gait.

43. Steppingstones look best when they project above the surrounding grade (about two inches). If the stones are thin, they may have to be set in a cement slush setting bed in order to hold them stable.

† *Ideas, principles and techniques taken from the* Sakuteiki

Moss and lichens on rocks and stone artifacts seem to link them more closely to the earth and the surrounding plantings—another illustration of the inseparable unity of *yin-yang. Hakusasonsō, Kyoto*

Both the sight and sound of the water action are enhanced by placing a splash rock beneath the lip of the falls. *Japanese garden, Westchester County, New York*

ROCK WORK IN JAPAN AND THE U.S.A.

Kyōto

Chisaku-in
Daitokuji temple complex:
  *Daisen-in
  Hōjō
  Hōshun-in
  Jukō-in
  Ōbai-in
  *Kohō-an
  *Kōtō-in
  *Ryōgin-tei
  Shinju-an
  *Zuihō-in
Entoku-in
Entsūji
*Ginkakuji
*Gosho (Imperial Palace)
*Hakusasonsō
Heian Jingū
*Higashi Honganji
*Hyōtei Restaurant, Nanzenji
*Katsura Rikyū
Kenninji
*Kinkakuji (Rokuonji)
Kitcho Restaurant, Tenryūji
Kurodani Kōmyōji
Myōshinji temple complex:
  *Taizō-in
  Tōkai-an
  Reiun-in
Murin-an
Nanzenji temple complex:
  *Konchi-in
  *Tenju-an
*Nijō Castle
Ninnaji
Nishi Honganji
*Ryōanji
*Saihōji
*Sanbō-in, Daigoji
*Shūgaku-in
*Tenryūji
*Tōfukuji

Other Locations

Fukudenji, Shiga Pref.
*Fuyō-en, Sakamoto, Shiga Pref.
Hōshaku-in, Shiga Pref.
Rakuraku-en, Hikone, Shiga Pref.
Renge-in, Sakamoto, Shiga Pref.
*Shiga-in, Sakamoto, Shiga Pref.
Kōshōji (formerly Shūrinji), Kutsuki,
  Shiga Pref.
*Asakura Estate, Fukui Pref.
Nan'yōji, Fukui Pref.
Makayaji, Mikkabi, Shizuoka Pref.
Tōkōji, Kōfu, Yamanashi Pref.
Tokushima Castle, Tokushima
En'yūji (former), Nagasaki
Negoroji, Wakayama Pref.
*Kiyosumi Teien, Tokyo
*Rikugi-en, Tokyo
*Kōko-en, Himeji Castle, Hyōgo Pref.

United States

*Gulf States Paper Corp. Headquarters,
  Tuscaloosa, Alabama†
*Missouri Botanical Garden, St. Louis,
  Missouri
*Japanese Garden, Japanese Garden
  Society of Oregon, Portland, Oregon
Tennessee Botanical Gardens,
  Cheekwood, Nashville, Tennessee
Hillwood Museum Gardens,
  Washington, D.C.
Nikko Hotel, Chicago, Illinois†

Highly recommended
†*Designed by the author*

Note: Although the gardens above
are generally open to the public, it is
advisable to check before visiting.
They may be temporarily closed for
repairs or special functions.

SUGGESTED READING

Japanese Gardens, Arts and Philosophy

Amanuma, Shinichi; Shigemori, Mirei; and Nakano, Sokei, eds. *Teien: Kyoto bijutsu taikan.* (Gardens: Kyoto art survey), Tokyo, 1933.

Asano, Kiichi, and Takakura, Gisei. *Japanese Gardens Revisited.* Tokyo and Rutland, Vermont: Charles E. Tuttle Co., 1973.

Covello, Vincent, and Yoshimura, Yuji. *The Japanese Art of Stone Appreciation: Suiseki and Its Use with Bonsai.* Tokyo and Rutland, Vermont: Charles E. Tuttle Co., 1984.

* Engel, David Harris. *Japanese Gardens for Today.* Tokyo and Rutland, Vermont: Charles E. Tuttle Co., 1959.

* Engel, David Harris; Seike, Kiyoshi; and Kudo, Masanobu. *A Japanese Touch for Your Garden.* 1986. Reprint. Tokyo: Kodansha International, 1992.

Hoover, Thomas. *Zen Culture.* New York: Random House, Vintage Books, 1978.

Horiguchi, Sutemi. *Katsura Rikyū* (Katsura Imperial Villa). Tokyo: Mainichi, 1957.

Ito, Teiji, and Iwamiya, Takeji. *The Japanese Garden: An Approach To Nature.* New Haven, CT: Yale University Press, 1972.

Kitamura, Fumio, and Ishizu, Yurio. *Garden Plants in Japan.* Tokyo: Kokusai Bunka Shinkokai (Society for International Cultural Relations), 1963.

Kitao, Harumichi. *Satei* (Teahouse gardens). Tokyo: Shokokusha, 1954.

Kubo, Tadashi. "An Oldest Note of Secrets on Japanese Gardens: A Compilation of the *Sakuteiki.*" *Bulletin of Osaka Prefectural University* (1956), B (6).

* Kuck, Lorraine. *The World of the Japanese Garden: From Chinese Origins to Modern Landscape Art.* Reprint. New York and Tokyo: Walker/Weatherhill, 1968.

* Murasaki Shikibu. *The Tale of Genji.* Translated by Arthur Waley. Reprint. 2 vols. Tokyo and Rutland, Vermont: Charles E. Tuttle, 1970.

Naito, Akira, and Nishikawa, Takeshi. *Katsura.*

Reprint. Tokyo: Kodansha International, 1994.

* Newsome, Samuel. *A Thousand Years of Japanese Gardens.* Tokyo: Tokyo News Service, 1953.

Nishimura, Tei. *Niwa to chashitsu* (Gardens and teahouses). Tokyo: Kodansha, 1957.

Niwa, Teizo. *Katsura Rikyū no tobi-ishi* (Steppingstones of the Katsura Imperial Villa). Tokyo: Shokokusha, 1955.

* Okakura, Kakuzo. *The Book of Tea.* Tokyo: Kenkyusha, 1940. Reprint. Tokyo: Kodansha International, 1991.

Oyama, Haruo. "The Japanese Coastal Landscape and Its Influence on Garden Design." *Yearbook of IFLA* (International Federation of Landscape Architects), 1992.

Ozaki, Hosai. *Right Under the Big Sky, I Don't Wear A Hat: The Haiku and Prose of Hosai Ozaki.* Translated by Hiroaki Sato. Berkeley: Stone Bridge Press, 1993.

Rito, Akisato. *Shinzen Teizo Den* (Report on a new selection of gardens). 1828.

Saito, Katsuo. *Niwa tsukuri* (Garden making). Tokyo: Kawade Shobo, 1955.

Saito, Katsuo. *Japanese Gardening Hints.* Tokyo: Japan Publications, 1969.

* Saito, Katsuo, and Wada, Sadaji. *Magic of Trees and Stones: Secrets of Japanese Gardening.* New York and Tokyo: JPT Book Co., 1964.

Sanders, Scott Russell. *In Limestone Country.* Boston: Beacon Press.

Shigemori, Mirei. *Kinki meien no kansho* (An appreciation of noted gardens in the Kinki Region). Kyoto: Kyoto Inshokan, 1947.

Shimoyama, Shigemaru, trans. *Sakuteiki: The Book of the Garden.* Tokyo: Town and City Planners, 1976.

* Slawson, David A. *Secret Teachings in the Art of Japanese Gardens.* 1987. Reprint. Tokyo: Kodansha International, 1991.

Tamura, Tsuyoshi. *Art of the Landscape Garden in Japan.* Translated by Sumie Mishima. Tokyo:

Kokusai Bunka Shinkokai, 1947.

Tamura, Tsuyoshi. *Jardin japonais: ses origines et caracteres: dessins et plans.* Tokyo: Kokusai Bunka Shinkokai, 1947.

Watts, Alan W. *The Way of Zen.* New York: Pantheon, 1957.

*Yoshikawa, Isao. *Japanese Stone Gardens.* Tokyo: Graphic-sha Publishing Co., 1992.

Yoshimura, Yuji, and Halford, Giovanna M. *The Japanese Art of Miniature Trees and Landscapes: Their Creation, Care and Enjoyment.* Tokyo and Rutland, Vermont: Charles E. Tuttle Co., 1957.

To rinsen meisho zue (Pictorial encyclopedia of notable gardens in the capital), Kyoto: late Edo Period.

Chinese Gardens, Arts and Philosophy

*Blofeld, John. *Taoism: The Road to Immortality.* Boulder, Colorado: Shambhala Publications, 1978.

Cao Xueqin. *The Story of the Stone.* Translated by David Hawkes and John Minford. 5 vols. Harmondsworth, Middlesex: Penguin Books, Penguin Classics, 1973–86.

Chi Cheng. *Yuan Yeh* (Landscape gardening). (Treatise with Foreword dated 1634) Beijing: Society for Studies of Chinese Architecture, 1933.

*Engel, David H. *Creating a Chinese Garden.* London: Croom Helm; Portland Oregon: Timber Press, 1986.

Giles, H. A. *Chuangzi.* London: 1964.

*Hay, John. *Kernels of Energy, Bones of Earth—The Rock in Chinese Art.* New York: China Institute in America, 1985.

Lin Yutang. *My Country and My People.* New York: John Day Co., Halcyon House, 1935.

Lin Yutang. *The Gay Genius: The Life and Times of Su Tungbo.* New York: John Day Co., 1947.

Liu Tunzhen. *Suzhou gudian yuanlin* (Classic gardens of Suzhou). Nanjing: Building Industry Press, 1978.

Mather, Richard. "Landscape and Buddhism." *Journal of Asian Studies* 17: 67.

Murphey, Rhoads. "Man and Nature in China." *Modern Asian Studies* 18: 67.

Pane, R. "Paesaggi e giardini cinesi." *Casabella* 304: 58-67.

Siren, Osvald. "Architectural Elements of the Chinese Garden." *Architectural Review* 10 (1948): 251-8.

*Siren, Osvald. *Gardens of China.* New York: Ronald Press, 1949.

Tung Chuin. "Chinese Gardens in Jiangsu and Chejiang." *Tien Xia Monthly* 3 (1936): 220-44.

Weng Wango. *Gardens in Chinese Art.* New York: China Institute, 1968.

* *Highly recommended*

WORKS CITED

Page 2 Musō Soseki. W.S. Mervin and Soiku Shigematsu, trans., *Sun at Midnight: Poems and Sermons of Muso Soseki* (San Francisco: North Point Press, 1989).
Page 5 Ibid.
Page 11–13 Hosai Ozaki, *Right under the Big Sky, I Don't Wear a Hat*, trans. Hiroaki Sato (Berkeley: Stone Bridge Press, 1993).
Page 13 Scott Russell Sanders, *In Limestone Country* (Boston: Beacon Press).
Page 15 Zong Bing. Quoted in Lorraine Kuck, *The World of the Japanese Garden* (New York and Tokyo: Weatherhill, 1968).
Pages 15–16 Bai Juyi. Ibid.
Page 16 Guo Xi. Ibid.
Page 16 Musō Soseki. *Sun at Midnight.*
Page 24 Lindley William Hubbell, *Seventy Poems* (Denver: Alan Swallow, 1965).
Page 34 Bai Juyi. Burton Watson, trans. (China Institute symposium, New York, 1985).
Page 36 Tao Hongjing and Li Bo. A.R. Davis, ed., *The Penguin Book of Chinese Verse* (Harmondsworth, Middlesex: Penguin Books, 1962).
Page 36 Matsuo Bashō. Harold G. Henderson, trans., in Harold G. Henderson, *An Introduction to Haiku* (New York: Doubleday, 1958).
Page 39 Matsuo Bashō and Onitsura. Ibid.
Page 39 Musō Soseki. *Sun at Midnight.*
Pages 41–42 John Blofeld, *Taoism: The Road to Immortality* (Boulder, Colorado: Shambhala Publications, 1978).
Page 46 Thomas Hoover, *Zen Culture* (New York: Random House, Vintage Books, 1978).
Page 104 *To rinsen meisho zue* (Pictorial encyclopedia of notable gardens in the capital) (Kyoto).
Page 105 Ibid.
Page 131 Shimegaru Shimoyama, trans. *Sakuteiki* (Tokyo: Town and City Planners, 1976).

Glossary

aware (Japn.) a pleasant pathos; a gentle melancholy; a poignant awareness of the transience of beauty.

block and fall pulley blocks with a rope or cable for hoisting or pulling.

cha-no-yu (Japn.) the Japanese tea ceremony.

Chan (Chin.) the Chinese term for Zen Buddhism.

chashitsu **(Japn.)** a room or tiny house designed for tea ceremony use.

chert a flintlike rock.

chōzubachi (Japn.) a high stone water basin, usually placed near the open veranda (*engawa*) of a Japanese house.

daimyo (Japn.) a Japanese feudal lord.

drumlin an elongated or oval-shaped hill of glacial drift.

engawa (Japn.) an outer veranda facing the garden in a traditional building.

fuzei (Japn.) an atmosphere, mood, or feeling; the evocation of an ambience by suggestion and abstraction, rather than faithful reproduction of a landscape feature.

geta (Japn.) a wood clog raised on two wood cleats. Traditional footwear in Japan.

Gosho the imperial palace in Kyoto.

Guilin a southern Chinese city famous for its karst limestone mountains. *See also* karst.

haiku (Japn.) a poem or verse in seventeen syllables generally relating to some aspect of nature.

hakusha (Japn.) fine, off-white gravel used in the raked "sand" gardens of Japanese temples. A natural rottenstone dug from the foot of a talus slope at Shirakawa, Kyoto. *See also* Shirakawazuna.

Heian Period the period of Japanese history dominated by the Fujiwara clan between the eighth and twelfth centuries. Vividly depicted in the novel *Tale of Genji*.

Hida Takayama a city in the Japanese "Alps" on central Honshu, the main island, famous for its sturdy domestic architecture designed to take heavy snowfalls.

Hideyoshi the supreme military leader preceding the advent of the Tokugawa Shogunate.

Higashiyama a mountain on the northeast side of Kyoto.

hōjō (Japn.) the abbot's quarters within a Zen Buddhist temple.

Horaisan (Japn.) the legendary island of Paradise.

ishi-dōrō a stone lantern.

Kamakura a seaside town south of Tokyo.

kameshima (Japn.) the mythic turtle island symbolized in Japanese gardens, it represents long life.

kami (Japn.) a god or spirit in Shinto.

Kangxi (Chin.) the Chinese emperor from 1661 to 1722.

Kansai the region around Osaka.

Kanto the region around Tokyo.

karesansui (Japn.) the dry landscape of the waterless gardens in Zen temples. Also applicable to any garden landscape with rocks and gravel suggesting mountains and water.

karst an eroded limestone landscape typical of Guilin, China.

Kasuga style (Japn.) the formal elaborated style of stone lantern. Often placed by the main ceremonial entrance path of a Japanese Buddhist temple or of a substantial home.

lang (Chin.) a roofed breezeway or path in Chinese gardens.

Laozi a Chinese philosopher of sixth to fifth centuries B.C. Believed to be the preceptor of Taoism.

longchuan (Chin.) an elegant Chinese porcelain made during the Song Dynasty (960-1279).

mizugoshi-ishi (Japn.) a rock placed in a stream to cause turbulence.

moraine the accumulation of earth and stones carried and finally deposited by a glacier.

nachiguro (Japn.) Japanese smooth, black, river-washed pebbles.

nobedan (Japn.) a broad, fitted stone pavement in a path consisting of both cut and natural stone pieces, often with mortar joints. A "stone carpet."

Ohaiyō-gozaimasu (Japn.) the greeting equivalent to "Good morning" in Japanese.

Qing the last Chinese dynasty (1644-1911).

revetment a facing of stone or other material to sustain an embankment.

Ryōanji the Zen Buddhist temple in Kyoto, famous for its "sand" garden of fifteen rocks.

sabi (Japn.) a term denoting several concepts: the mellow patina of age or wear; ancient, serene, subdued, possibly with sad tones of loneliness.

samurai (Japn.) a soldier-warrior during Japan's feudal centuries.

sanzon (Japn.) a triad; a triangular composition of rocks viewed either vertically or in plan.

sasa (Japn.) dwarf bamboo planted as edging or ground-cover.

schist metamorphic crystalline foliated rock that splits along parallel lines.

sensei (Japn.) a teacher or mentor. The term applies to a master or expert in a profession or an art.

shakkei (Japn.) borrowed scenery; a view of distant scenery incorporated into a garden composition.

shibui, shibusa (Japn.) quiet; composed; elegant; under-stated; astringent.

shigaraki (Japn.) a pottery with a wood ash glaze produc-ing rustic, unpredictable drip effects in browns, yellows, greens. Kilns in Shiga Prefecture.

shinden-zukuri (Japn.) an architectural style prevailing in houses of nobility during the Heian Period. Characterized by pavilions facing south and connected by roofed corri-dors.

Shinto the native Japanese animistic cult predating Buddhism.

shirakawazuna (Japn.) another term for *hakusha*, the fine off-white gravel which is raked into swirls and patterns.

shogun (Japn.) a military ruler, especially of the Tokugawa Period.

shōji (Japn.) a paper screen in a wood frame which serves as a sliding panel separating two spaces.

Shumisen (Japn.) another term for the mythic isle of Paradise.

Song the dynasty which ruled China 960-1279.

suiseki (Japn.) a miniature stone landscape in a tray.

sute-ishi (Japn.) small rocks disposed in a Japanese garden as if thrown randomly, helter-skelter.

swales a low-lying or depressed stretch of land that drains away water.

tachigata (Japn.) a tall, upright stone lantern, as opposed to the low, squat types.

taihu (Chin.) a type of convoluted, pierced limestone rock found in Lake Taihu, China.

Tang the dynasty which ruled China 618-906.

Tao the Way; the philosophical basis of Taoism.

Taoism the ancient Chinese mythic animistic philosophy of individual liberated life affected by exaltation of nature.

tate-ishi (Japn.) rocks set in an upright position.

Tianshan a mountain range in northwest China.

ting (Chin.) a Chinese garden pavilion, kiosk or gazebo.

tobi-ishi (Japn.) steppingstones in a Japanese garden.

Tokugawa the clan who established the Shogunate which ruled Japan from the sixteenth century till 1868.

tsubo-niwa (Japn.) a small garden adjoining a building.

tsukubai (Japn.) a low-set water basin.

tsurushima (Japn.) the rock arrangement denoting "crane island" in a *karesansui* garden.

wabi (Japn.) deliberate restraint and understatement; the illusion of poverty and artlessness; rustic solitude; melan-choly, lonely, impoverished, humble by choice, calm, quiet.

yin-yang (Chin.) the two opposite yet complementary components of reality, such as the male-female duality.

yūgen (Japn.) a poignant foreboding; obscurity; mystery; suggestiveness.

Zhuangzi (Chin.) believed to be a follower of Laozi and a preceptor of Taoism.

INDEX

A high mountain

soars without

a grain of dust.

A waterfall

plunges without

a drop of water.

Once or twice

on an evening of moonlight

in the wind

this man here

has been happy

playing the game that suited him.

—Musō Soseki